SHOWING

SHOWING

JANE HOLDERNESS-RODDAM

First published in Great Britain by
Kenilworth Press
Addington
Buckingham
MK18 2JR

First edition 1989
Second (revised) edition 1997
Paperback edition 2004

British Library Cataloguing in Publication Data
A catalogue record for this book is available from the British Library

ISBN 1-872119-79-4

Line drawings by Dianne Breeze
Design by Paul Saunders
Layout by Kenilworth Press

Printed and bound in Singapore by Stamford Press

PHOTO CREDITS

All photographs are by Anthony Reynolds, with the exception of the following:
John Birt 12, 14, 15, 34, 80, 81, 84, 85, 89 (bottom right)
Cherry Wilde 17, 32, 33, 46 (left)
Bob Langrish 26 (bottom), 146, 160

CONTENTS

PART 1 – SHOWING AND RINGCRAFT

PART 2 – GUIDELINES AND REFERENCE CHARTS FOR INDIVIDUAL CLASSES

PREFACE

THIS NEW AND REVISED EDITION of **Showing** has been thoroughly updated to help showing exhibitors gain as much useful information as possible about the vast number of classes available in which to enter their exhibits.

The book, which is divided into two parts, covers general aspects of horse care, training, presentation and general ringcraft necessary to show your horse off to its best advantage in the ring. It also includes useful advice on how to make the most of your animal's attributes, as well as how to avoid some of the pitfalls. Guidelines on dress and presentation for exhibitors, judges and stewards are also included. For the first time, this edition also features a section on unaffiliated shows, as well as information on Sport Horses and Veterans' classes.

In Part 2, useful reference charts provide an invaluable quick guide to over a hundred different classes covering most of the popular classes in today's showing world. These cover whether the judge rides, the accepted tack and turnout, whether an individual show is expected, etc.; and the accompanying text tries to give an overview of each type or breed mentioned.

It must be borne in mind that fashions and trends change and one can never keep totally up-to-date, so it is essential to keep in touch with what is going on in the area in which you are particularly interested by checking carefully in the relevant schedules, as well as with the different societies or breeds, as appropriate.

I have tried to incorporate answers to all the numerous questions I regularly get asked, and very much hope the book helps you to benefit from what, I am sure you will agree, is an extremely rewarding and enjoyable pastime.

JANE HOLDERNESS-RODDAM

ACKNOWLEDGEMENTS

THE AUTHOR WOULD LIKE TO ACKNOWLEDGE with grateful thanks the assistance she received from numerous people in the revision of this book.

In particular, Richard and Marjorie Ramsay for all their help and advice with the material and photographs; also, Mrs Sue Nichol and Andrew Nichol, Mrs Pamela Montague-Hall, Mrs Frances Hutchinson, Charlotte Fry, Mrs Marion Knapfield, Mrs Helen Horton and Mrs Rose Bourne for giving up a day to help with photography; Mrs Jennie Loriston-Clarke, Mrs Anne Dicker, Mrs Pam Harvey Richards, Mrs Ursula Roberts, Miss Tessa Clarke, Edward Hart and Carol Morse for their helpful advice.

She would like to thank Pauline Henson, Karys Westcott and Sandra McCallum for their typing, research and patience with the manuscript, and Lesley Gowers for her persistent but understanding prompting throughout. Also Anthony Reynolds, who took most of the photos for the book, and Dianne Breeze for her line drawings.

She would also like to thank all the various organisations listed in the book for their helpful advice and assistance, both for this and the previous editions.

1

Showing and Ringcraft

CHAPTER 1

An Introduction to Showing

WHAT IS A SHOW HORSE?

Perhaps the show horse can best be described as the most nearly perfect example of the type or breed of animal it represents. In ridden classes it must also perform in the correct manner for the class. The best overall exhibit is the one that will catch the judge's eye.

CONFORMATION

Conformation plays a very big part in the show animal. However, the overall impression is likely to be the deciding factor at the end of the day.

- The head is probably the most important feature and must be in proportion to the rest of the body and pleasing to the eye. In certain classes it will have to conform to rules for that particular type. The way it is set on to the neck and how it is carried will be noticed by the judge, and the whole bearing and presence of the horse seem to be governed by the head.
- The neck should be nicely muscled and come out from well-shaped withers. It should be in proportion with a good top-line and not have an over-developed bottom line. The neck should not be set on too low, i.e. coming out of the shoulders, and should be nicely curved. The arch of the head and neck is the crucial factor in defining presence, which is so important in the show horse.
- The back should be strong and well proportioned, neither too long nor very short. It should be well muscled and the rider of the ridden show

OPPOSITE: Winning a first-prize rosette is everybody's dream!

The show horse should be an outstanding example of its breed or type and perform according to the rules relevant to its class.

horse should appear to be sitting in the middle so that the overall picture looks in balance.

- The quarters should be strong and rounded, and well muscled on top and between the hind legs. Hind legs that are 'split up the back' indicate weakness, as do quarters which slope away from the backbone. When seen from behind, the horse should give a strong and balanced view on either side.

- The shoulders should be sloping with plenty of freedom. The saddle should sit well back behind the shoulder with the shape of the body allowing for this. A very straight shoulder indicates lack of freedom, resulting in a short or choppy stride and often an uncomfortable ride. A 'stuffy' or 'overloaded' shoulder will usually offer the same restricted movement. Look at the horse from the front to ensure there is some width between the front legs; they should not 'come out of one hole'.

- The body should be rounded and well proportioned so that shoulders, body and quarters all join up well together. The ribs should be well sprung and rounded, giving the horse 'depth' or a 'good girth'. A shallow horse indicates weakness.

- The limbs – 'bone' is the essential element and this is the deciding factor in hunter or weight-carrying classes. Bone is measured just below the

Remember
If your horse is a good mover with only reasonable conformation it may still have a chance in the show ring; this is when presentation becomes even more important.

knee, round the cannon. It should be flat in preference to being rounded. The smaller, finer breeds may be rather light in this respect but it is the overall picture of proportions that should be considered.

- The knees should be strong and flat. Shorter, rather than longer, cannon bones denote strength. The cannon bones should be hard and flat with the tendons well defined and the fetlock joints flat rather than too rounded. Fleshy-looking legs with very rounded 'apple' joints are not favoured. The pasterns should be gently sloping; upright pasterns cause a 'jarring' action, and those which slope too much denote weakness.
- The hocks should be a pair, strong and straight. They should have a good angle without too much bend, indicating weakness. If they are too straight, mobility may be restricted. There should be a definite angle between the hip, stifle joint and hock for good movement of the hind limbs.

Remember
It is quality rather than quantity that is required, and no show should take longer than one and a half minutes if done professionally.

Hunters are one of the most popular show classes and here we see three happy riders following the championship prize-giving. Note the plain double bridles and ratcatcher tweed jackets.

- The feet must be well shaped and in good condition. Good shoeing, with the right shoe for the occasion, is very important. Many a horse with doubtful action has been greatly improved by careful corrective shoeing, so don't completely discount an animal who has, for example, a slight 'dish'. Discuss the matter with your farrier to see what can be done to improve it. The judge, however, will be looking for perfection so the horse with the fewest problems and faults is likely to come out on top.
- The overall picture should be pleasing to the eye and the animal must have that extra something which makes it stand out from the others. The quality that says 'look at me', known as presence, makes the world of difference to the show horse and often it is this which catches the judge's eye long before the proportions and conformation have been assessed.

Colour

There is no doubt that good strong colours catch the eye. Rich bays, browns and chestnuts seem to head most of the line-ups with grey also being a good colour for the show horse. Wishy-washy colours do not stand out, so a horse of indifferent colour needs to be really good in other respects to be noticed. In some classes colour is essential to the type and is

Ponies need to perform in a manner suitable for their young riders - well behaved at all times and schooled for their appropriate classes.

Before and after a good trimming session! You need a good eye to be able to see a pony in the raw and visualise it when correctly presented.

assessed on its quality. For example, palominos are expected to gleam like a 'newly minted gold coin' and only a minimum amount of dark hairs are allowed in the mane and tail.

Good markings as well as a good colour can accentuate looks: a central star or stripe, or a pair of white socks or even four white legs, can look magnificent on a show horse whereas they might be less favoured in other fields of competition, such as in eventing or jumping where white legs are sometimes prone to sensitivity. One white leg, sock or stocking can slightly unbalance the picture, especially if it is in front, and likewise a pair of feet of the same colour is preferable.

Remember
If your horse has a good frame, is in good condition and is well presented for the class, you have a real chance of being noticed.

Movement

The movement of the horse plays a very big part and can often compensate for minor conformation defects. A good mover can rise several places in the final line-up. The rhythm and stride, as well as straightness, are what count so it is extremely important that the animal is allowed to show itself off to its best advantage by its rider or handler. In some classes, such as those for Welsh Cobs, it is essential that the handler can run briskly, as the cob is expected to move at a very strong trot in front of the judges to show off its naturally inherent movement.

The type of movement should be reflected by the category of horse or pony being shown. While a hunter would be expected to have a good strong trot, be able to show some extension and also to gallop well, the elegance of the hack should be reflected in its paces. In breeding classes the quality of the movement is important. The current trend is to be more selective with regard to movement.

MANNERS

The way of going and manners are very important assets in the show horse. Children's ponies, hacks and riding horses, in particular, are expected to be perfectly behaved at all times, but all horses, whatever their type or breed, must perform well throughout. Any horse or pony considered by the judge to be not under proper control or ill-mannered, is likely to be asked to leave the ring.

In-hand classes can sometimes become a recipe for disaster with strong two- or three-year-old colts taking charge of the proceedings. Discipline is

A happy combination sharing that winning moment in an in-hand class.

REMEMBER
Judges are nearly always pushed for time and a short, sharp show will be more appreciated than a longer one.

important from an early age, and firm handling is essential for youngsters if they are not to become a danger to everyone, including themselves. It is quite unacceptable to show animals which cannot be controlled, and excuses are simply not good enough. Any horse or pony out of control is potentially dangerous and should not be brought out in public until it is sufficiently disciplined to be able to behave reasonably.

Horse and handler running in step – always quite an art to achieve, but it helps to show this lovely horse off to its best advantage.

The individual show

The individual show is the one chance the rider has of presenting his horse or pony to the judge without the distractions of the rest of the class, so it is essential to make the best possible use of the brief time available.

- The judge will expect to see that the animal has a reasonable walk, so a few strides should be shown before moving into trot, which, if possible, should include some extension. A canter, including a change of rein to show both leads (if time permits), plus a gallop if appropriate to the class, followed by a halt and rein back, and/or canter on to a final halt complete the show. Be aware, however, that trends change, so watch the classes in which you are interested to see what is popular and expected.

The ride

The ride by the judge in such classes as hunters, hacks, cobs, riding horses and ridden breed classes, can have a considerable influence on your horse's final placing, so good training and manners when under saddle are very important. Make sure that your tack is suitable for the judge to ride in, and check that the stirrup irons and leathers will fit him/her – problems here will not help towards promoting your horse's good points as a ride.

- The hunter and cob must give a good workmanlike feel with a positive free-moving performance and be able to really stride on at the gallop, pull up and stand still.
- The hack must be beautifully trained and an easy, light ride capable of being ridden 'on the little finger'. It must be responsive, collected and well mannered, and particularly suitable as a lady's ride. Hacks are not expected to gallop but must be able to stride on well, pull up easily, rein back and strike off on either leg. The riding horse should be similarly trained but should gallop on and be a lovely, easy, handy ride capable of doing anything and going anywhere.
- Children's ponies must be exceptionally well mannered and obedient with smooth, easy paces. They should be an easy, straightforward ride, suitable for the age of the child rider.
- All the mountain and moorland breeds are hardy tough animals but their rides should be light and easy with comfortable strides. They should be able to gallop on and come back to a halt, and whatever their size they should feel well proportioned and balanced, and have impeccable manners.

Running up in hand

Running up in hand offers the judge a good opportunity to study your horse close-to and see how straight and well it moves. How you present your horse will very much influence the judge's assessment. The horse or pony must therefore be taught to stand up properly, not take long to adopt a good position and obediently step forwards or backwards as required to give the judge the best possible view. It must lead out well and show itself off at the walk and trot, moving freely and actively to give a good outline. Knowing how to make the most of your horse in this phase is essential to success.

In sport horse classes, which are becoming increasingly popular, the running up in hand normally follows the Continental triangular pattern. Practise leading your sport horse in this way so that both of you are used to it – you need to be quite fit!

Remember
Try to be objective about your horse and if after two or three times in the show ring it still remains far down the line, it is best to ask a professional about its future prospects, or admit defeat and try it in another role.

Faults

While some faults may go unnoticed at smaller shows, they will not be overlooked at the bigger, affiliated shows.

- Curbs, spavins, thoroughpins and obvious ring-bones or side-bones will definitely go right down the line. Splints are tolerated by most judges so long as they are not unsightly and do not interfere with the action of the horse, but the horse without a splint will generally be put up if a judge has to choose between two otherwise equal exhibits. Capped hocks are unsightly; they are not a conformation fault, but more a management problem.

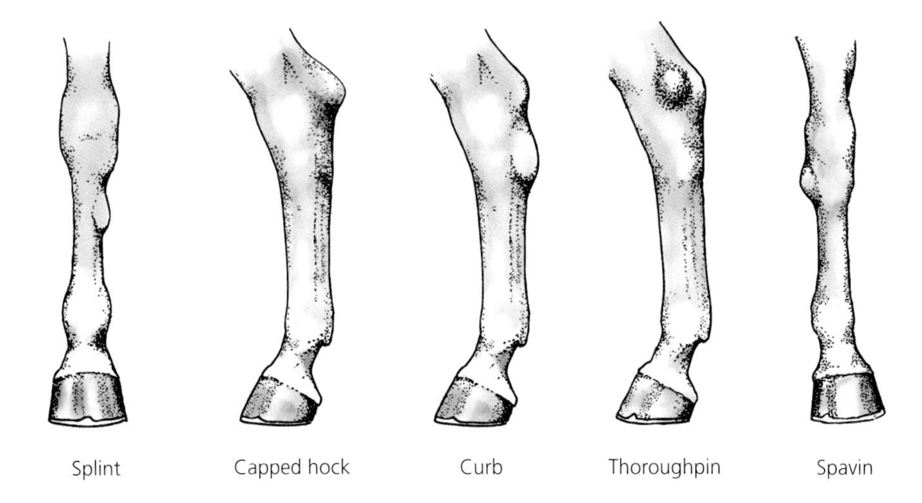

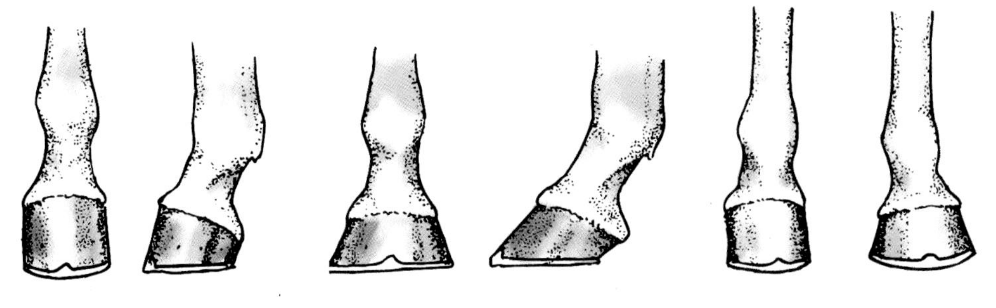

Boxy feet   Flat feet   Odd feet

The goose-rumped horse usually has a low-set-on tail. it is not generally favoured but may indicate a good jumper.

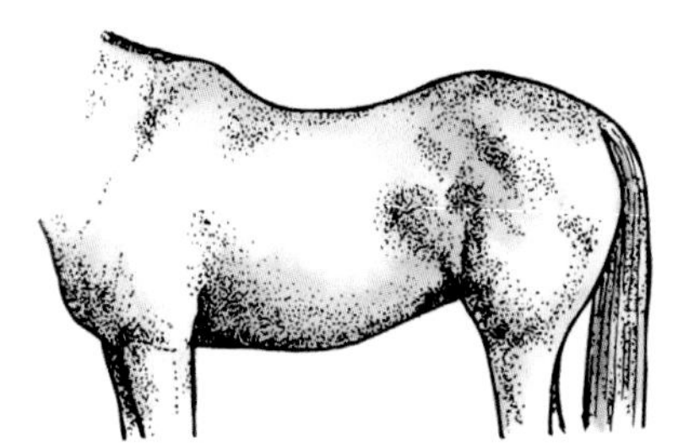

Dipped, hollow or sway backs may be strengthened by giving all feeds on the floor. They are rarely noticeable until the horse is stripped. Keep the horse's head low when in front of the judge, and work on correct schooling to build up as much muscle as possible.

A roached back is difficult to disguise; a horse with such a noticeable fault will never be a success in the show ring.

Ewe or weak necks can be improved with careful strapping, feeding and schooling. Clever plaiting on top of the neck will help disguise this problem.

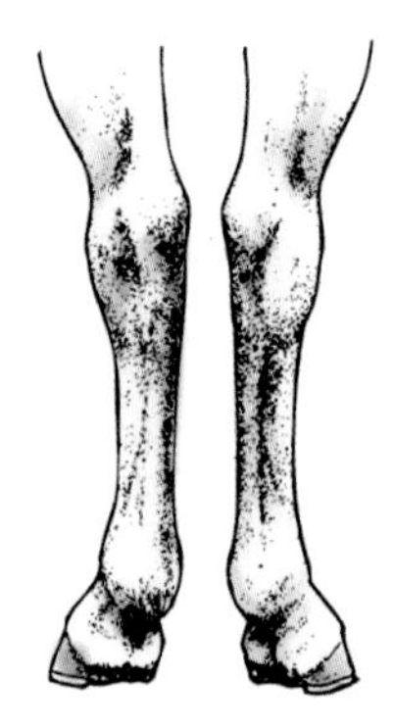

Cow hocks are a conformation defect. The farrier might be able to improve mild cases with corrective shoeing. Don't stand the horse up square behind in front of the judge.

- Animals with roached backs, dipped backs, ewe necks, very short necks or very large heads will not make show horses. Those with cow hocks, sickle hocks, club or odd feet, contracted heels, crooked legs and any obvious signs of unevenness such as a dropped hip and a badly crooked spine, will also never make it in the show ring.
- Horses that have been operated on for wind or that have been fired or pin-fired are barred from many classes judged under official society rules, but they may compete in unaffiliated shows and it is left to the judge's discretion as to whether or not to penalise them; inevitably if there are two horses of similar standing the horse without a problem should beat the other.

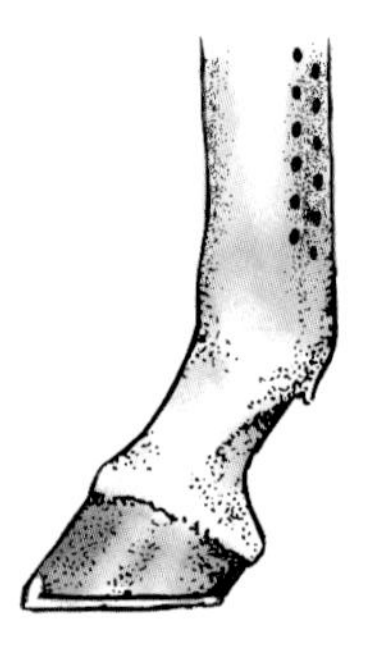

Pin-fired

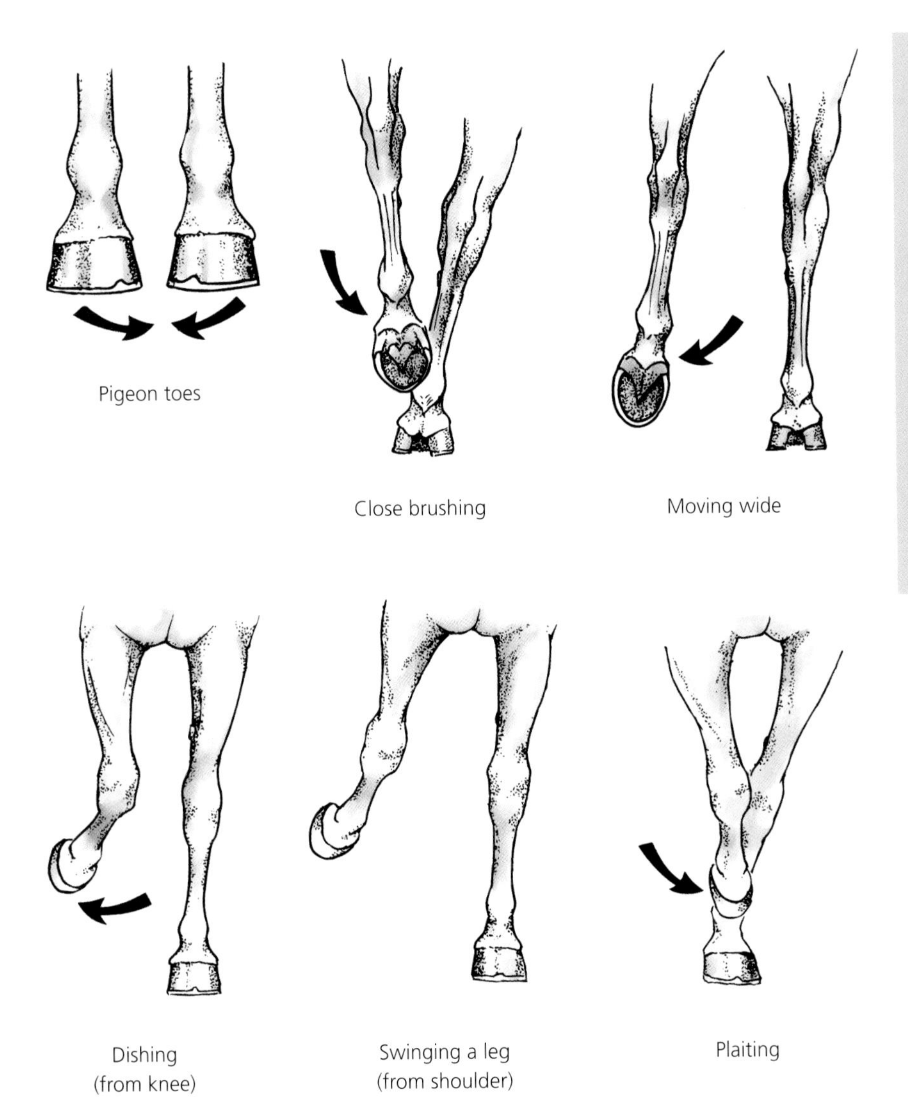

Remember
There are some horses that will never make a show horse for various reasons, such as those with conformational defects, faulty movement (e.g. bad dishers) or bad manners, although the latter should be correctable with proper training.

- A horse which moves badly will also be at a distinct disadvantage. If your horse 'dishes' noticeably, turns a foot in, swings a leg, goes very close or 'plaits', and shoeing cannot help, then he will usually end up lower down the order after being run up in hand. There have been many handsome horses that would have been champions had they moved better, and there have been champions whose magnificent movement has helped judges to excuse their other faults.

CHAPTER 2

Health and Condition

The general health and condition of the show animal are vital to its success in the ring. When it comes to your horse's general management, attention to detail is what counts.

- Peak condition of the show horse must be the number one priority, so a thorough **worming** routine must be established. No horse will thrive if carrying a worm burden. Ask your vet what worming programme he would recommend.
- **Flu and tetanus vaccinations** are generally compulsory at the larger shows and many showgrounds insist on seeing your horse's vaccination certificate. Make sure yours is up to date and corresponds with the requirements. The new passport regulation (2004) should ensure that these are current. Ensure details have been transferred, if necessary.
- **Teeth care** is another important consideration, both to ensure that the horse can masticate properly and obtain maximum benefit from its food, and to help keep it comfortable in its mouth so that it goes well without any sharp teeth causing discomfort and encouraging head tossing and general aggravation. It is sensible to have the horse's teeth examined by a vet or equine dentist twice a year and rasped as necessary.

FEEDING

The show horse is required to look well rounded and a picture of health throughout the showing season. Overfat animals cannot move properly, and in the past many youngsters were ruined by being overfed too young, resulting in all sorts of growth problems. If your horse is to have a hope of reaching his full potential he should be allowed to mature at a natural rate.

Feeding the show horse is a great art. Travelling will take its inevitable toll, particularly if you do a lot of showing, but you have to keep the condition on without letting the animal get out of hand or over-fresh. There is no doubt that a **daily spell in the field**, in a safe, well-fenced paddock, **will help tremendously to relax the horse and give him some green food and sunlight, which is always beneficial.** A relaxed horse will always thrive much better than a highly strung one.

Keeping the fibre content above 50% is important. Most show horses would be best kept on a diet of 30%-40% concentrates/60%-70% fibre.

What to feed very much depends on what you are used to and on the individuals concerned but the following have been found to be particularly useful for the show horse.

- **Barley** is good for show horses and is higher in energy but lower in fibre than oats. Micronised or extruded barley is preferred as it is clean and easily digested, having been through a special heat process which breaks down its hard exterior. Barley is also very good fed as a boiled feed mixed with a little linseed, which will enhance the coat.

- Any **boiled food** is more easily digested and is a great 'pick-me-up'; it is usually a firm favourite with most horses. Some people boil oats as well as barley, mixing in **linseed** which is extremely appetising and excellent for the coat. Some people give boiled food with mashes once a week, others feed boiled food every day.

- **Oats** are useful for those horses who lack sparkle in the ring, especially young animals and ridden youngsters who easily tire. They are high in fibre.

- There are several specially made **coarse mixes** designed to suit horses in different types of work. Some mixes are specifically designed to be non-heating and to cater for different types of animal and are extremely popular for the show horse.

- **Sugar-beet pulp** is excellent for fattening but should be used with caution as it has a high energy content. It can therefore be used to provide the sole source of energy if fed with chaff or alfalfa.

- **Bran** and **chaff** make useful fillers but bran should only be used in moderation as it is now known to interfere with the balance of calcium and phosphorus if fed in large quantities. Bran mashes with Epsom salts once a week can act as a laxative, preventing a build-up of food. Most chaff is often fed mixed with molasses and/or herbs in some form or other, which is excellent as an appetiser and high in all sorts of minerals, vitamins and trace elements. Molasses also come in meal or syrup form, when they can be added to the feed or mixed with warm water to dampen it.

- **Maize** is a very good fattening food which is not too heating. It is usually fed flaked and is found in most proprietary mixes. It is low in fibre but higher in energy than oats or barley. It is excellent fed with alfalfa.
- **Oil** is most important in keeping the coat shiny and glossy and whilst there is adequate oil in most mixes, the addition of something like cod liver oil or sunflower oil is excellent for encouraging a little extra sheen. It also provides energy, so adjust the horse's concentrate ration if necessary. Feeding two tablespoons up to a quarter pint daily should be enough to make a difference, but always check for an underlying cause if your horse's coat looks poor.
- **Linseed oil** is also excellent for the coat and many people feed it mixed with boiled barley.
- You might decide to feed some sort of **supplement** if you are doing a lot of showing. Choose one which seems right for your horse or stable and stick to it – don't become one of those people who give a mass of different supplements and extras, since most will either double up on the same ingredients causing an imbalance or simply be a waste of money. Some supplements are high in oil, so check this before feeding extra oil to the feed. Others contain biotin which, when mixed with calcium and zinc, may improve hoof growth. Probiotics help boost healthy bacterial action in the lower gut, so improving effective digestion.
- There are many excellent **herbal supplements** and remedies on the market, such as chamomile and valerian, which are reputed to have a sedative effect; thyme and lavender, which are natural antiseptics; and peppermint and garlic, which have fly repellent properties.
- Good quality **hay** is particularly important and should make up between 60 and 70% approximately of the show horse's diet. Whether it is hard or soft hay matters little so long as it is of good quality, clean and sweet-smelling. Alternatively, there are several varieties of vacuum-packed haylage available, which are excellent (but higher in protein). These products are useful for the horse who has a dust allergy, otherwise soak the hay and drain well before feeding. Alfalfa and chaff are also good sources of fibre.

- Tasty trimmings from **carrots**, **potatoes** or **chopped cabbages** are often much appreciated and add variety to the diet. Freshly cut grass is also excellent, especially when it is not possible to turn the horse out.
- The type of **water** your horse drinks can make quite a difference to its coat. Soft water definitely seems to impart an extra glossy and soft silky shine. Take care, though, if you are changing from one type of drinking water to another as some horses have been known to show signs of colic.

GENERAL HINTS ON FEEDING SHOW HORSES

- Adjust your feeding programme to suit the individual. No two horses will respond to the same feed in exactly the same way.
- Feed little and often. This is especially important with a fussy feeder and will help him to keep condition on. Some horses prefer small feeds anyway, finding large feeds rather off-putting.
- Feed at regular times as much as possible. The horse is a creature of habit and does not respond well to change.

EXERCISE

- **Turning out** is an excellent way of providing exercise and relaxation. Used in this way it is just as important as riding and schooling, and by turning out, the danger of making the animal too fit is avoided. Most show animals would benefit from being ridden for half the week and turned out for the other half, or being ridden and then turned out for a few hours every day.
- To protect against knocks and bruises while in the field and to protect the coat, many people put on boots all round and a turnout rug.
- **Lungeing** is a useful way of exercising and can be done either loose on a lunge line and cavesson or with side-reins attached to the bit. Many show horses tend to become very one sided because they spend more time going round the show ring on the right rein, so lungeing provides an excellent opportunity for working them on the stiffer side.
- Youngsters from two-year-olds upwards can be lunged a little on either rein as part of their education.
- **Long-reining** may be more appropriate for youngsters as there is no

A spell in the field does wonders in maintaining health and condition – as proven by this 32-year-old veteran. Boots may be advisable if your horse is likely to injure itself.

strain on any particular side of the body and it teaches them to go forward from the start, to accept the bit (which should be a simple rubber or rounded snaffle) and to get used to the roller or saddle. Those that have been well long-reined are little trouble when it comes to backing later on. They can be driven round fields or tracks for experience. Long-reining can be used on all types of horses and ponies and may help their way of going when ridden, particularly those who do not go forward and tend to drop behind the bit. However, do be sure that your hands are soft and light at all times.

Long-reining can be a very useful form of exercise and schooling, both for the young horse or to improve the way of going of older horses.

- All horses and ponies will require a certain amount of schooling relative to their intended classes, and for ridden horses this should be interspersed with hacking out. Training and schooling is dealt with in the next chapter.

Shoeing

Shoeing is most important, and how your horse is shod may be reflected in how well and straight your horse moves. Regular checks on how your horse moves and attention by your farrier on a routine basis will pay dividends.

- Light shoes are recommended for the lighter types such as ponies, hacks and riding horses. Aluminium plates will encourage them to have a lighter action but most other animals are shown with light- to middleweight steel.
- **The farrier can often do a tremendous amount to help a horse with doubtful action and to disguise bad or odd-shaped feet.** Talk over the options with him but be sure that a long-term effect is your ultimate aim – short cuts could be seriously detrimental to the horse.
- Your farrier can also advise on the use of **studs**. Many show riders fit them to prevent slipping in the ring, especially in those classes where galloping is expected. Large studs are inadvisable on very hard ground but can help considerably in wet conditions.

Keeping the show horse well rugged up is very important in maintaining a good coat. Make sure it is well-fitting so that it does not cause any rubbing.

GROOMING

Grooming is another essential chore which will greatly influence the general appearance of the show horse. A well-groomed coat stands out, and although there is no doubt that some horses have especially good glossy coats without seeing a brush too often, the majority will benefit from a good daily grooming routine.

- A **body brush** can be used all over, but use the hand to rub round any sensitive areas, such as the ears, elbows and under the tummy of the sensitive horse.
- A **rubber curry comb** is extremely efficient at loosening the hair once the coat is starting to change. Used in a circular motion it can be taken all over the body and is very helpful on both the insides and outsides of the legs.
- A **wisp** (nowadays many use the leather pad variety rather than the old hay type) may be necessary on animals that are not well developed on their necks and quarters. **Strapping** on a regular basis may help to enhance these areas but the secret lies in banging slowly, allowing time for the muscles to contract and then relax before the next bang. Done in this way the muscles are really made to work, but if the movement is too fast the correct effect is lost. Strapping should not be done on youngsters.
- **Care of the mane and tail** comes into play during daily grooming, and damping and laying the mane over to the right side should be a part of the session. A good brush through, including the forelock, will encourage the mane to remain neat and tidy. The tail should be damped down well and a tail bandage applied for a few hours a day to ensure it stays looking good. Remember to remove the bandage before settling your horse for the night.
- An unruly mane can be improved by occasional plaiting over. It must be well damped first and should not be left plaited for more than twenty-four hours or the hairs will tend to break. 'Pull-on' type hoods can be quite effective as mane layers so long as the mane is pushed well over to the right side underneath.
- A lot depends on how well the mane and tail are pulled in the first place. If the tail is to be plaited the hairs should be as long as possible if it is to look really neat. Never brush out the ends of the tail as this can remove hairs and eventually ruin the appearance of the tail. Separate the hairs

by hand if possible, or take hold of the tail firmly and brush out the ends on show days only.

- A **stable rubber** is the most important part of the grooming kit; use it to give the coat a final polish. If used every day after grooming it will help to keep the coat fine and remove particles of grease which come to the surface. Coat-shine products or oil rubbed in two or three times a week may be beneficial.
- **Hoof care** should be carried out daily, with careful picking out of the hooves and a good oiling, inside and out, three or four times a week in hot weather when the feet tend to dry out. Applications of cod liver oil are excellent for keeping the hooves in good condition. More conventional hoof oils can be used when the horse goes on an outing. Rub oil well into the coronet band to keep this in good condition, as it is from here that the foot grows. Any rough or torn bits of frog should be tidied up by your farrier.
- The **chestnuts** on the horse's legs must be kept neat and tidy. These should be peeled off regularly and not allowed to grow too large. If they have become very big and tough your farrier will be able to pare them down to a manageable size; you can then keep them in good shape on a weekly basis when grooming.

USEFUL TIPS ON GENERAL MANAGEMENT

When considering the health, condition and day-to-day management of the show horse, the following points may help towards preventing unnecessary mistakes:

1. Feed the horse adequate food to keep condition on but do not overdo the energy intake so that he becomes unmanageable. Keep the fibre content up.
2. Give the horse adequate exercise to keep him calm and sensible. Do not overdo the work or he will become fitter and fitter and may get out of hand. Turn him out or loose lunge him occasionally to give him the chance to buck and kick and to relax.
3. Keep the animal well protected when out on exercise. **Blemishes of any sort are not favoured in the show ring.**
4. Make sure that there is adequate bedding so the horse does not get scuffed or capped hocks when he rolls or lies down in his stable.

All horses will benefit from some relaxing hacks in the countryside. Riding out also helps them to become accustomed to different sights and sounds. Note the protective boots.

5. Keep your horse well rugged up to ensure that he keeps his summer coat until the end of the season.

6. Teach the horse to lead and stand up properly from the word go, and be sure this is done properly when you lead him in and out of his stable. Practise standing him up, as if for the judge, two or three times a week.

7. All riding horses must be made to stand still while you mount and they should remain standing until you ask them to move off. This way they are seen to be well mannered when mounted in the ring by the judge.

8. Plan your worming routine, shoeing and teeth care to suit your showing programme. It is inadvisable to have your animal shod the day before a show just in case the farrier shoes him a bit tight, making him go a little uneven for a day or two. Have the shoeing done a few days beforehand to allow time for any problem to settle down.

9. Make sure that your show horse has been ridden by other people before entering him in a show class where a judge is to ride. Some horses may have been ridden by just one person and it is unfair to the judge if he ends up being the one to discover that your horse does not take kindly to strangers. Some young horses may find the weight or size of different riders unusual.

Chapter 3

Training and Schooling

The training of the show horse or pony is crucial to its success. The judge wants to see your horse's best performance straightaway, whether the animal is being led in hand or ridden. Any exhibit that fails to please at the moment when it has the judge's attention is liable to be ignored, however perfect its conformation. **It is therefore up to the exhibitor to present the horse in front of the judge in such a way that a favourable assessment can be made.**

Requirements for in-hand classes

In-hand classes are difficult enough to judge at the best of times so it goes without saying that your horse must lead properly. You should walk at its shoulder and the horse must walk forward well, keeping its head straight so that its movement is not spoiled.

While some horses can be led in a neat headcollar it is usual for broodmares to be led in a double bridle and stallions in an in-hand show bridle with a snaffle. Youngstock usually have an in-hand bridle, but with a rubber bit or a neat show cavesson and coupling with a leather or white-webbing lead rein. Heavy horses are often shown in halters, as are some of the native breeds. The emphasis must be on control first and foremost. Make sure you practise at home and are confident that your horse is controllable in the tack you intend to use at the show.

Some stallions can become a bit of a handful at a show, or just not show themselves off too well, without side-reins. These are quite acceptable in most cases and will keep the horse's head straight so that it will move well. Practise running up in-hand with side-reins on, ensuring that they are only

The way you stand up your horse in front of the judge is vital. Practise at home and always stand in front, encouraging the ears forward to produce a good overall impression.

tight enough to keep the horse under control and in balance but in no way restrict it.

Foals must be led properly and should be kept close to their mothers. They must learn to stand still while the dam is walked and trotted back in hand. They must also learn to walk up and trot back quietly beside the dam. Straightness is what is being looked for when the judge asks for a trot-up, so try to ensure that all animals, regardless of age or size, go **straight** – this is the first lesson to be learned.

Standing the horse up in hand is the most important moment in the class. Practise thoroughly at home, teaching the horse to move into position quickly and to stand up well. While some breeds require a particular stance most classes call for the animal to stand so that the judges can just see all four legs. **The horse should stand naturally**, being neither too stretched out nor too 'bunched' together, and straight when viewed from the back or front.

The neck should be nicely arched at a suitable height to make the horse's head and general bearing look its best. The ears should be pricked to complete a good picture from which the judge can make his choice. Picking up a handful of grass in the ring or giving a polo may produce the desired effect on the day, but don't practise this routine at home too much or it may lose its impact.

Ensure that your animal responds quickly to being pulled forward or pushed back a step so that it is in the right position when the judge inspects it, and also that it leads away straight and turns away from you when you turn to trot back straight. Don't allow it to misbehave or become out of control; likewise be sure it is not idle, so that you have to drag it along.

Requirements for ridden classes

The ridden horse must be perfectly mannered in every way. You must be sure to ride it in company quite regularly so that you know it will behave at a show. Make certain it is used to other horses overtaking and will not, above all, kick out.

- Children's ponies must be well behaved in all respects but particularly when other ponies are coming up close behind, as children are notoriously bad about looking where they are going. Ponies should be forward-going and obedient but in no way strong for the child. Leading-rein ponies should be manoeuvred as much as possible by the child with very little help from the handler. They should show willingness and active responses while in no way being too jerky, quick or sluggish.

- Hacks and riding horses must be beautifully schooled, showing collection and extension, halt, rein back, and strike-offs on a given leg, and riding horses must be able to gallop.

This youngster has been well trained to trot up in hand with confidence and is producing a very pleasing picture overall.

Schooling at home must include appropriate work for the type of class entered. The show hack, for instance, must be beautifully schooled on the flat, while the working hunter pony needs to perform confidently over all types of fences.

- Hunters and cobs must be good workmanlike rides going forward into the bridle well, comfortable on both reins and really able to stretch out and gallop. They must pull up well, halt and stand still.

- Ridden native ponies and riding pony stallions must go nicely at all paces, be comfortable and obedient and be well schooled. Even a Shetland, if well trained, can be a lovely ride, despite its size. Ponies tend to be a bit 'mouthy', probably because they are often ridden by children, who are apt to treat them a bit like a toy and pull away at their mouths. It is worth spending a little time in finding the best bit and schooling the animal carefully before entering a class.

- **Training the rider** is just as important as training the horse, as ultimately it is very much up to the rider to show off the horse. When schooling the horse it is worth making the rider do a show periodically and having a practice in a field with other horses. For horses or ponies that are going to be ridden by the judge this is a good time to practise putting other riders on board.

- **Children need to be taught how to ride an individual show and must learn not to ride too close or too far away from the judges.** They must be taught as much as possible, but not to the point where the lessons become a bore. This is very important if the younger generation are to enjoy themselves and continue showing.

- Working hunters and working hunter ponies, which will be required to jump a course of fences, must be trained up to the necessary standard. Most of these courses are rustic, and some include a combination fence which involves a turn for the second element, as well as some sort of water jump or ditch.
- Be quite sure that you have thoroughly trained the animal so that it can jump a reasonable grid, will go well round a cross-country course and is confident over a set of show jumps. Equipped with this sort of all-round experience most animals should be capable of jumping the average working-hunter course. Working-hunter courses should be jumped at a fair hunting pace, and a good flowing round is expected. Too often problems arise because riders will not get straight for the fences to give the horses the best chance, so this must be instilled into the jockey.
- **Galloping** plays an important part, especially in hunter classes, but riders very often hold their horses back instead of really letting the judge see how they can move. While galloping is not something one should overdo, it is up to the rider to show that the horse can stride out well. Sit up and ride the horse forward in front of you, then pull it up. The horse will look its best galloping with its head up and out a little, and it should look and be controlled throughout. At home practise on both reins as the judge might want to ride the gallop in both directions, so the horse should be equally handy on the right and left leg.
- The **walk** is the pace shown during the final parade before being pulled into place, so ensure that your horse or pony looks good and walks out well. A horse with a stilted and restricted pace will not be favoured any more than one that is slopping along with its head on the floor. Look at the horse yourself or ask a knowledgeable person to watch you ride the horse to see how it looks its best. **A good rhythm and flowing stride should be the aim, with the head being well carried and the horse in self-balance.**
- The **halt** needs regular practice. Neither the rider nor judge (if appropriate) will appreciate having to haul away at the horse in an effort to stop it. Schooling should be such that the horse responds immediately and can come back to a halt when required, from any pace. It must then stand still and remain so, even if the rider decides to drop the reins on the neck, until asked to move forward. This is most important as it is

often the way a judge might assess manners in the class.

- **Mounting** and **dismounting** are other times when manners may be observed, and, here again, the horse must remain still. It is absolutely essential to teach the horse to stand and be obedient from the very beginning. Many professionals train their horses to stand still by themselves to impress the judges. Remember, the horse is a creature of habit and will learn quite quickly, provided you enforce the habit every time using the same words to indicate your wishes, such as 'whoa' or 'stand still'. Practise mounting from the ground as well as being given a leg up so that the horse is accustomed to both methods.

- **Reining back** is usually required in show pony, hack and riding horse classes. It is an indication of good training, so spend some time perfecting it. The animal should step back straight with lightness and ease. Correct training will be required to show this important movement, which is often followed by a strike-off into canter, accentuating the degree of training reached. It is best not to rein back at all until your horse is sufficiently well schooled, and likewise not to attempt it on a young horse until it is quite settled in the ring. **Timing is always one of the secrets of success and to ask for a rein back when the animal's eyes are almost out on stalks at its first show will probably result in the reaction such stupidity deserves.** Practise at home first, then try out your training at a small show before taking the plunge in front of all the stars. **In showing, it is better not to attempt a particular movement at all than to perform it badly.**

- The show animal must not spook or misbehave in any way, so it makes sense to take it on frequent outings and ride it about to see the sights so that it becomes quite used to all the varied and often quite alarming sights of the show world.

- If you can enter a variety of different classes so much the better, as this will help check any desire to anticipate the usual pattern of a certain class. Many animals learn the routine of walk, trot, canter and tend to get strong in readiness for the gallop. Attempting something different, such as a dressage test, which any well-schooled show horse should be more than capable of, will vary the scene a little. Side-saddle riding may well offer another outlet for your horse's talents, as may the equitation classes.

- **Side-saddle** is something that requires practice at home. While it is usually unnecessary to do this too often, both horse and rider will benefit from a few schooling sessions to perfect the way of going. Check that the saddle is a good fit and have it checked over regularly. The rider must be sure to sit up straight and square, and the horse should go forward straight and respond to the rider's aids quite happily. It may be necessary to sharpen up the horse's responses on the right side by using a long dressage whip so that it learns to understand that the whip is taking the place of the leg. Be sure to take care of the horse's back and harden it up with surgical spirit if necessary. If the rider is sitting correctly and the saddle fits properly there is rarely a problem. Depending on whether you are doing equitation classes or ladies' hacks, hunters or side-saddle on ponies, practise until you have the horse going just as it should in all paces.

LOADING AND TRAVELLING

One aspect of training that must never be forgotten is ensuring that your show animal will load into the horsebox or trailer without a problem. Nothing is more frustrating than a horse who will not load. Most starts for shows are inevitably quite early, and the last thing you want to discover is that you have failed to check up on this vital element of training.

- Youngsters, in particular, should be made to go in and out of the box periodically, and if difficult, given their feeds inside until they are confident and happy about it. A couple of trial runs are sensible also, to be certain that you are not going to have problems on the big occasion.
- Protect the show horse well, particularly over knees, hocks, head and tail, which are all vulnerable to injury on the journey. Injuries are certainly going to wreck the show horse's appearance, quite apart from reducing its value.
- Most animals settle quite quickly as long as they have some hay to nibble at, but there are a few who are rather neurotic about being cooped up in a horsebox. Be extra careful with any who may start trying to climb out, and never leave such animals unattended in case they get themselves into trouble. Perseverance is what matters, so set aside a few mornings to practise with the horsebox so that your day at the show will be less stressful!
- Some animals get quite desperate if left looking out on the surrounding scene. With cases such as these it is advisable to keep the windows and ramps closed until they settle. This problem is usually short-lived and disappears as outings become more familiar.

A poll guard is a sensible precaution when travelling a very big horse or a youngster liable to play up when in the box.

- Taking another experienced horse along for company to the first couple of shows can be helpful, but remember to take the youngster out of the box first, so that it doesn't become hysterical, thinking it has lost its friend. Loading the schoolmaster first will give confidence to the youngster.
- Firm and sensible handling is required to ensure that your horse is a pleasure to take around rather than a menace, so tackle this part of the training early and overcome any problem before it escalates.

WHAT NOT TO DO WHEN TRAINING THE SHOW ANIMAL

1. The show horse or pony must enjoy its work so that it 'shows off' to the judge and looks happy with its ears pricked. If you ever lose this look you have basically lost your show horse, so it is important not to overdo showing. Sourness can set in if the horse is dragged from show to show with little variety in its life outside the ring. Overshowing can also lead to anticipation in the ring so that the horse tries to take over instead of only performing as and when asked.
2. Never overfeed your horse so that it becomes overloaded and gross.
3. Make quite sure the horse is well protected throughout his training so that he does not knock himself and become blemished; protect him well when travelling.
4. Never allow bad habits to set in. The horse must behave all the time and any misbehaviour must be treated firmly straightaway so that it does not develop into a problem. At the slightest indication of any problem treat the cause immediately. Nappiness, coming out of the line, kicking out

at others, behaving badly and not standing in line, must all be dealt with either with a sharp reprimand or extra work, according to what would be best for the individual's character. The secret is to nip the problem in the bud.

5. Youngstock must be well trained at home before they are taken to a show, yet, despite training, they can still be naughty. These animals really do need firmly controlling at all times as they can easily become a danger to the public, to you and to themselves. Make it quite clear from the start that you are the boss.

6. Know what you are aiming for. Watch the professionals, see how they do things, then perfect the art at home in readiness for the big occasion.

Parades can be daunting, especially for in-hand youngstock, as they involve quite a lot of standing around and preparation before entering the arena. Be alert for all eventualities and accustom your show horse to being among others whenever possible.

- The final walk round is a fairly critical time as this is the occasion, particularly if the class has galloped, that manners show up. Be sure to relax yourself at this time – a few deep breaths may well help the two of you to remain calm. Don't let your horse become idle; keep him walking up to the bit and attentive all the time.
- Don't look directly at the judge but watch out of the corner of your eye to see if you have been called in. Many are the times a rider has failed to notice and then been missed out altogether.

THE INDIVIDUAL SHOW

If you have to do a show it should be short, sharp and give a really good impression of how well your horse is trained. A walk, trot and canter, showing a change of rein and striding on (or a gallop as appropriate), a halt, rein back and a still halt on a loose rein will show all the judge needs to see. How you do this is up to you, but the shorter the better. **It does not take long for an experienced judge to assess a well-trained horse so remember that 'short is beautiful' as far as your show and the judge is concerned.** The judge will take into account obedience, way of going, and acceptance of the bridle.

RIDING BY THE JUDGE

When your horse is to be ridden by the judge, dismount in the line-up and quickly ensure that the leathers are approximately the correct length. Be certain to keep the horse warm before and after he is ridden so that he does

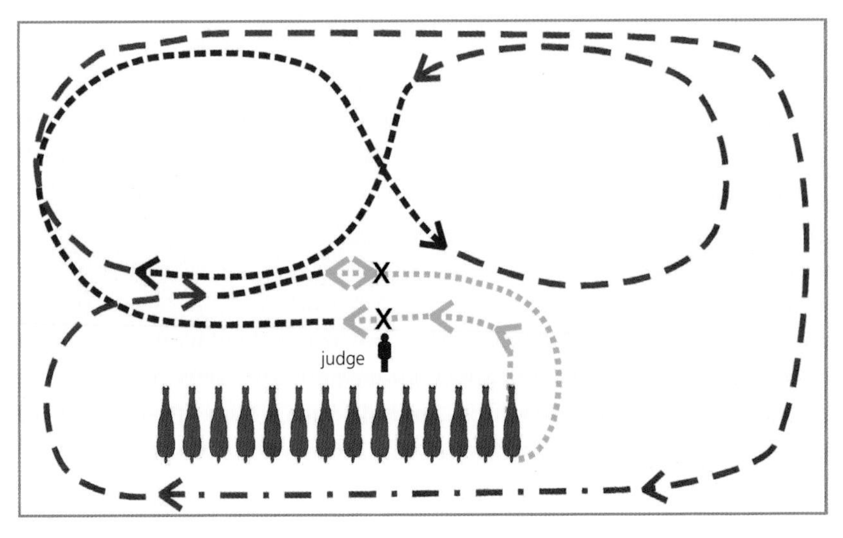

A simple show with figure-of-eight and gallop, suitable for children's ponies, riding horses and hacks. The gallop is optional.

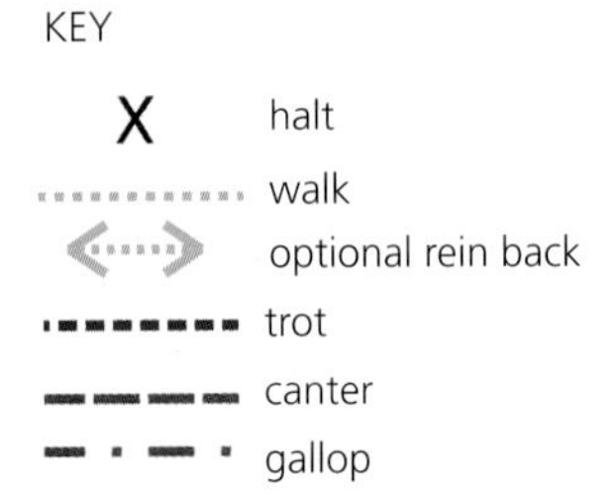

Most judges prefer a leg-up from the steward, but your horse should be used to being mounted from the ground as well. Make sure your stirrups have been adjusted to the appropriate length and ideally your horse trained to stand still during mounting.

not get a cold back and his coat stays looking good. Put a sheet over him if it is very hot to prevent the coat standing up on end.

Don't be disappointed if the judge stays on board for a very short time. If he obtains a good feel straightaway and likes the horse he will not waste further time on it. Of course, if he doesn't like it at all he may also get off as soon as possible, so you may be none the wiser either way! **The important thing is that the animal behaves and goes calmly and obediently.**

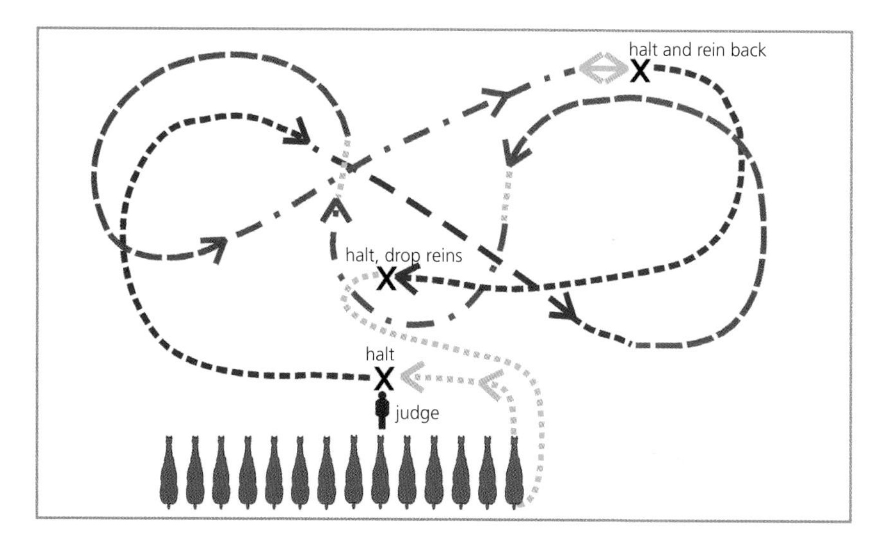

A more advanced show with change-of-rein loops, halt and rein back, and showing extended trot and canter. Suitable for hack and riding horse classes and pony championships, etc.

KEY

X halt
walk
rein back
trot
extended trot
canter
extended canter

The judge will want to assess your horse from every angle and may well move the tail aside to assess the hocks. It is important that your horse is well mannered and used to this type of handling.

RUNNING UP IN HAND

- When the horse is stripped, make sure your groom quickly flicks off any saddle or sweat marks and be ready to walk up as the last horse in front of you is being shown.
- Stand the horse up correctly a little away from the judge on (if possible) a flat piece of ground. Stand in front of the animal holding the reins, which should not drag on the ground. Smile at the judge as you check that the horse is standing up properly. Pluck a little grass to encourage your horse to prick his ears and arch his neck.
- If the judge moves round to view from the other side re-position the horse if necessary and then lead him up at the walk, push him away from you to turn, and then trot straight back towards the judge and on past him so that he can see your horse's action. With a slightly doubtful mover, the clever rider may move on past in a curve to help disguise this shortcoming!
- In certain classes movement can play a very important part and handlers of heavy horses, Welsh cobs, etc. need to be able to run fast to show their horses properly in hand. If you can't do this yourself make sure you have a suitable person ready to lead on these occasions.

TIP
Accept defeat gracefully – there's always another day.

- Some sport horse classes require you to trot the horse around in a triangular pattern to see it from all directions (see diagram, page 114). Make sure you and the horse are fit and able to do this.
- Always be sure you know what stance is required for the different classes and teach your horse or pony to stand accordingly. **To be professional you must produce the required goods.**

SIDE-SADDLE

For side-saddle classes, whether ponies, hacks, hunters, etc., make sure your helper is in the ring early enough to help you dismount. Before you do so, remove the elastic loop which keeps the skirt down in place, from around the toe of your boot. Then ensure that the skirt is folded round the back to become an apron and buttoned under the jacket so that it looks neat and tidy. Adjust the stirrup to suit the judge if appropriate.

When remounting, be sure to tighten girths correctly – don't rush this important part of tacking up, even if the rest of the class is waiting; however, do be as quick as you can.

GENERAL TIPS ON RINGCRAFT

1. When riding in the ring, don't fall into any of the traps which tend to catch the unwary, but do make sure you are seen by the judge.

A line of cobs showing the accepted tack and turnout for this strong, tough type of horse. Remember to have a suitable length and size of stirrups to fit the judge who will ride the exhibits in this class.

TIP
Missing a class is very easy, especially with youngsters. Keep an eye on what is happening, listen for announcements and be prepared at all times.

2. Never get into a bunch, especially in front of the judge. If you keep your wits about you it is quite possible to avoid this situation by using the ring sensibly.
3. Be careful of the unsporting competitor who will come on your inside just as you are about to trot beautifully in front of the judge.
4. Sit up, look professional and really show your horse off at all times.
5. Carry your show cane in the middle so that it is nicely balanced in your hand. In hack classes it is an indication of good manners and training to ride with one hand, resting the end of your cane on your thigh. If carrying a hunting crop be sure that you hold it so that the head is facing down. The leather thong must have a lash on the end. In side-saddle classes longer whips are permitted. It is correct to hold a cutting or neat dressage whip up at the top.
6. When galloping, either sit up well or fold forward and ride the horse strongly in front of the judge. Don't be one of the nervous types who won't let the horse go. Avoid being overtaken – this is the time when horses play up. It is usual to gallop only once past the judge.
7. Don't get too close to other horses; some may be at their first show and quite unpredictable. Treat every horse with suspicion and you are then likely to avoid an unnecessary kick.
8. Look at the horses in the collecting ring and if possible avoid following the most outstanding horse when actually in the ring as it will only overshadow your own. First impressions are important, so get out there, assert your position and don't hold back.

BELOW: Competitors waiting for their class. Be sure you are ready on time.

BELOW RIGHT: It is inevitable that you need to overtake other riders at times, but do this away from where the judge is looking, such as along the back of the ring or cut across a corner, but never be unsportsman-like and do so in front of the judge.

9. Try to avoid getting stuck behind a horse that is misbehaving; give it a wide berth so that it does not upset your own mount, and find another slot.

10. If your horse is rather spooky or nervous, don't go too close to the outside of the ring where there tend to be all sorts of hazards and distractions. Stay just on the inside so that he will be more relaxed.

11. Sometimes young horses get quite fidgety when standing in line for long stints. It may be best to dismount. Playing with the bit, taking a packet of polos into the ring or giving him nibbles of grass will probably help him settle.

12. It looks extremely unprofessional to be seen smoking in the ring. Likewise, wandering up and down the line chatting to friends is equally undesirable. If you have other exhibits in the ring then walk discreetly down the back of the line, but if possible send your groom.

    You should stand beside your horse while dismounted during the class and your groom should stand quietly behind the horse once she has finished tidying him up. The less that is seen to be done the better it looks.

IN-HAND CLASSES

For in-hand classes the exhibits must be well behaved at all times, but with several youngsters perhaps on their first outing, this is not always easy to achieve. Some good exercise the day before is a wise precaution as any equine playing about is a danger, not only to the public but to you and the animal as well.

- **Be certain that the leader or handler is experienced and strong enough to cope with a youngster.** A docile broodmare is one thing, her exuberant one-, two- or three-year-old quite another. The well-behaved foal may be quite a different animal with its new-found independence and strength a year later.
- Neatness and tidiness in the ring, for both horse and leader, is a must – jeans, T-shirts, skimpy tops, shorts or frilly dresses are not the corrrect wear for the show ring.
- **Wear suitable footwear which allows you to run up your horse safely and easily**, and always carry a show cane.
- Standing in line with some youngsters or stallions can be a little un-

Very neat and tidy turnout for showing in hand. Note the sensible shoes that will enable both handlers to run their charges up in front of the judge.

nerving. Keep an eye on your animal all the time. Don't stand too close to others, and if you have any problems be firm straight away.

- **With stallions and colts keep a discreet eye out to ensure their sheaths are not showing.** If a colt draws in line, walk him around at the back until he settles. Don't allow him to run round in circles but keep him occupied in some way. If in a mixed class you find your colt next to a filly, stand him a little in front and keep his attention throughout so that he does not get bored and naughty. It is not difficult to keep colts and stallions under control if you are observant and command their respect.

THE ROLE OF THE GROOM

- The groom is very important to the show exhibitor and is responsible for keeping the animal looking its best throughout the class.
- Grooms should take as little as possible into the ring, but the bare essentials are a sponge, stable rubber, body brush, hoof pick and oil, and show sheet or rug, depending on the weather. In very hot weather the horse's coat will tend to stand up, so a sheet should be placed over the animal. In cold weather the same may happen as the horse tends to get chilled while standing in line. A day rug will keep the horse warm and should be put on as soon as possible.

The role of the groom in the ring is vital if your show horse is to be presented in front of the judge looking its very best. Grooms should be neat and tidy and carry a smart rug and grooming kit.

- Grooms are usually allowed into the ring after the exhibits have been lined up. They should stand quietly behind their horses and do only the minimum. They should not be seen giving the horse a full-scale grooming session in the ring, but should quickly tidy up as necessary. In ridden classes the groom or rider must alter the stirrup length to suit the judge.
- Once all the exhibits have been seen by the judge and the rider is remounted the groom should leave the ring as unobtrusively as possible. Grooms should also enter this way, being sure not to get in the way of anyone performing a show.

WATCH THE PROFESSIONALS

When at a show, take every opportunity to learn from what you see. Look at those at the top of the line, and then at those at the bottom. Try to glean as much as possible about the requirements for that particular class. Look at how the professionals are turned out; notice what tack is used and how the horses are trained. The most professional people seem to do very little but still manage to have their exhibits looking just right – without appearing flashy they look the part, being neat in every respect, well presented, well behaved, and stand out as very worthy winners. Try to follow their example.

CHAPTER 5

Formalities

REGISTRATIONS, MEMBERSHIPS AND CERTIFICATES

Although usually unnecessary at small shows, at affiliated shows animals have to be registered with the relevant breed society or association which governs the rules and regulations for that particular breed or type of class. It is usual for both the exhibitor and horse to be registered, as well as the rider, annually. This will involve filling in an identification form and, where relevant, a Joint Measurement Scheme certificate may be required as proof of the animal's height. Make sure you get this done in plenty of time and arrange it through your veterinary surgeon.

If your horse is likely to be near the height limit, work him hard the day before measuring and ask your farrier to trim his feet right down. A bran mash the night before will help to keep him calm, which is the main point to bear in mind.

Arrive at the measuring station with time for the horse to relax. Encourage your vet to give your horse the time he needs. Keep the horse's head low, in line with his withers and allow him to 'flop'. Some horses will sink down as much as 35–50mm (1½–2 ins) if they are given time to relax. Make sure that he is standing square and not bunched up in any way.

IMPORTANT
Many societies no longer express horse and pony height in hands. Be aware that centimetre equivalents are becoming the norm.

Membership and registration numbers often have to be quoted on entry forms. It is important that you think about this early enough so as not to miss out on the early shows. Most societies run their memberships from 1 January. If your horse or pony is registered with several societies keep your records carefully and take a photocopy with you to shows, in case of any query on eligibility for a class or special rosette. Many societies require armbands to be worn to indicate that you qualify for special awards. Organise these now so that you have them for the day of the show.

TABLE OF HEIGHT CONVERSION FROM HH TO CENTIMETRES

12 hh	=	122cm	14.2 hh	=	148cm
12.2 hh	=	128cm	15 hh	=	153/154cm*
13 hh	=	133cm	15.1 hh	=	155cm
13.2 hh	=	138cm	15.2 hh	=	158cm
14 hh	=	143cm	15.3 hh	=	160cm

** Check the class rules carefully for this measurement as the conversion may vary in each society's rule book – for example, the NPS and BSPS use 153, whereas the BSHC&RHA uses 154.*

Flu vaccinations

Nearly all big shows now require a valid certificate of flu vaccination with a diagrammatic description of the horse.

Don't leave checking your flu vaccinations until it is too late. Always make a note of when boosters are due so that you don't miss the date and have to start the whole procedure again – a very expensive mistake.

Prohibited substances

Read through the lists of prohibited substances issued by the various societies which affect you. Ensure that the feed you are giving is declared free of offending ingredients in case you are ever drug-tested. Fly sprays sometimes contain forbidden substances. It is your responsibility to ensure that you are legal. If you are at all unsure, it is safest to change to another brand of food or spray.

Entries

When making entries, be sure to read all the details concerning your classes. Some class numbers are subdivided into groups, especially in youngstock classes, so be sure you have put yours into the right section for his age, height, etc. Write clearly and legibly so that the details appear correctly in the catalogue on breeding, breeder, age, colour, etc. Check if any armbands need to be worn to show that you are eligible for special awards, and put this down on your entry form if required. Enclose any necessary details regarding memberships or registration numbers for the current year and copies of vaccination certificates if required. Send the correct amount in entry fees, and for stabling if required.

Keep a note in your show entry book of exactly what you have requested with stabling, along with your list of entries. Always ask for sufficient passes – you may end up with a problem if you arrive with three people and only two passes. Some shows require a stamped self-addressed envelope for the return of numbers and passes, so be sure to supply one if this is the case. At other shows you may have to collect your numbers from the secretary on arrival, so give yourself adequate time. **Don't forget to take with you all the show information and numbers if these have been sent out in advance – and remember, any armbands for special awards may have to be made up in the appropriate colours.**

CHAPTER 6

Dressing for the Show Ring

Having the right tack and clothes is essential if you want to look professional in the show ring. Remember, though, it is the animal that is being judged, not you; your clothes should be neat, tidy and well fitting, and, above all, should not detract from the horse.

CLOTHES FOR THE RIDER

What you wear depends on the class being judged. It is considered very unprofessional to be seen wearing the wrong clothes for the class, and even worse to be over-dressed, so study the form and ensure that you are properly attired and complement your horse.

- Neatness and tidiness are the two most important factors. Collars and ties should look and be neat, with a tie-pin securing everything in place. Some people fasten the points of their collars with a tie-pin for added neatness. If hunting ties (or stocks) are to be worn they should be well tied and not too bulky. They should be secured with a plain stock-pin and large safety pins to keep the ends in place to prevent them coming out. The stock-pin should be worn straight across horizontally unless it has a small figure on it, in which case it can be placed diagonally. It is both incorrect and dangerous for the pin to be worn vertically.
- Children's jodhpurs should be a good fit, with an elastic loop sewn into the bottoms so that they stay neatly down over the jodhpur boots. They should be a good neutral beige or cream colour, and not too bright for working ponies.

In hack and riding horse classes, overalls and top hats are worn by men in the afternoon at Royal shows or in the evening indoors.

- Breeches should be well fitting, and for hunters and cobs a neutral beige colour. Cream is usual for the more showy classes, such as for hacks, riding horses and ponies.
- Hunting boots, usually black, should be a good fit and not too short in the leg. They should look smart and be beautifully polished. Garter straps should always be worn with the buckle on the outside of the knee.

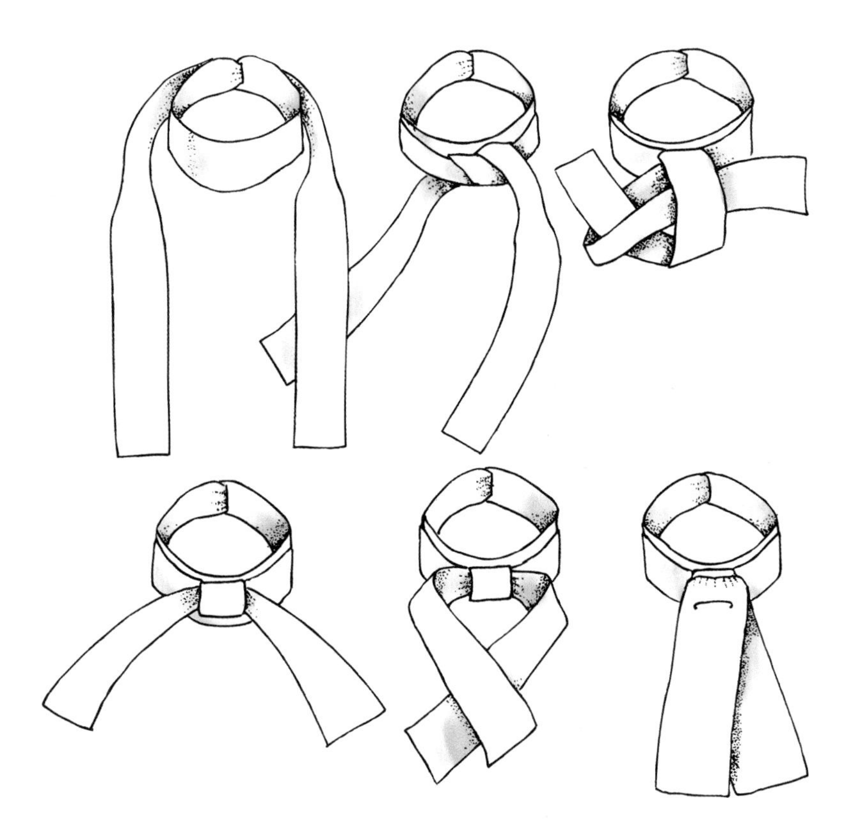

Tying a hunting tie. A neat end-result, with the knot well covered, and a plain stock-pin placed horizontally (never vertically), is correct.

Old-fashioned breeches used to have buttons sewn just below the knee, through which the garter strap was passed. These are seldom seen today. Modern boots tend to be shaped at the top and no longer have garter straps. Brown boots can be used with tweed coats, but never with blue or black ones.

- Jodhpur boots, usually worn by younger children, may be black or brown but must be spotlessly clean.
- Spurs are correct turnout for most adult classes and should always be worn with hunting boots. The curve of the spur must point downwards, and the spur-strap buckle should be on the outside of the boot with the point of the strap pointing downwards. Both spur and buckle should be polished. Spurs are not permitted in children's classes. For those who do not wish to ride in spurs, a dummy type without a shank at the back can be worn instead.
- The jacket should be neat and tidy and fit well. It should not be too short in the body or in the sleeves. Tweed jackets should be unobtrusive

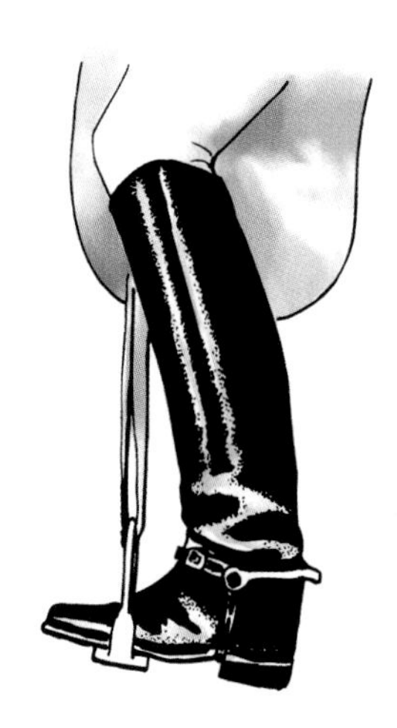

If spurs are worn,they should always be worn with long boots. (Judges, of course, should never wear spurs.) A garter strap, buckled on the outside, should be worn with a hunting boot but not on a boot with a shaped top (as shown).

Incorrect: fancy stitching and shaping is incorrect for showing and the spur is far too low on the heel.

Jodhpurs and jodhpur boots are correct for all children's classes. Neatness is ensured with the attached fastening keeping the jods pulled down over the boot. Note the safety stirrup with rubber loop which will snap should an accident occur.

Incorrect: gentlemen's top boots should always be worn with spurs and white garter straps.

without a strikingly obvious pattern or check. Two or three buttons at the front and the same on the opening of the lower arm are correct. Black or navy blue jackets (brown is also acceptable for children) should be well fitting with no obvious or bright-coloured lining.

- If a buttonhole is worn it should be small and neat and on no account be large or effusive. Buttonholes are not worn with tweed coats.
- Earrings are inappropriate and look unprofessional.
- Usually a hat with a safety harness or a skull cap with a velvet cover is compulsory for all children's classes, mountain and moorland classes and in adult working hunter classes. Hunting caps, top hats and bowlers may be worn if rules permit.

  Hats should be black or navy blue. (Sometimes children wear a brown cap with a brown jacket.) The cap should be worn so that the peak is horizontal to the ground. Hair should be neatly tied back, bunched or plaited for girls, and neatly tucked away in a hairnet for ladies. It is very incorrect to have hair coming out under the brim of a hat or to have the hat placed on the back of the head.
- Bowlers should be worn square to the ground, and ladies should have a neat bun at the back. They are worn with a collar and tie and a tweed coat; they are also seen with black and blue habits for side-saddle riding, worn with a veil.
- Top hats are only worn for finals or in evening show classes. A hunting tie (stock) is always worn with a top hat. For ladies, a veil is used with a

A well-polished plain boot with a dummy spur. These are ideal if you do not want to wear one with a shank. All spurs should fasten on the outside of the foot with the end of the strap facing to the rear.

Two different but very neat hairstyles, note the different colours of harness – either of which are correct but it may be worth making a decision on which is most suitable for the overall picture.

Two types of hats worn with veil for ladies' side-saddle classes. The bowler is worn with a collar and tie and the top hat with a hunting tie (or stock) is appropriate for afternoon and evening performances at Royal shows.

top hat for side-saddle classes. It is correct to wear a bun, false if necessary, with a top hat.

- At Royal shows in the afternoon, or evenings for finals and championships, correct hunting attire is worn for hunter and cob classes. The correct dress for men is a plain or cut-away black or scarlet hunting coat, top hat, hunting tie, with white breeches and top boots with white

The trimmed 'round' number generally fits better and looks tidier than the square option.

Two well-presented riders dressed in ratcatcher, suitable for hunter, working hunter and cob classes, as well as unaffiliated shows.

garters for a scarlet coat, or beige breeches and plain boots for a black coat. For women, a plain blue or black coat, fawn breeches, plain hunting boots, hunting tie and top hat are appropriate. A hunting whip or show cane should be carried and, as always, spurs should be worn with long boots.

- For evening wear in hack classes, a frock coat, overalls and top hat are worn by men for finals and championships at major shows, accentuating the elegance of this type of horse. Women wear top hats and blue or black coats.
- Gloves should be worn at all times. Pale string gloves should be worn

A picture of elegance. Both the rider and judge look immaculate, not to mention the horse. Note how the judge's skirt is looped round and buttoned at the back when she is not riding.

with full hunting dress. Brown leather gloves are worn with tweed and blue or black coats and for side-saddle riding.

- The show cane, either Malacca or leather-covered, is carried for all show classes and should be a comfortable size, length and thickness for the

Three different types of cane suitable for show riding. They should, however, be held a little more towards the centre to be really correct. This could be important in an equitation or best rider class where every little detail is scrutinised.

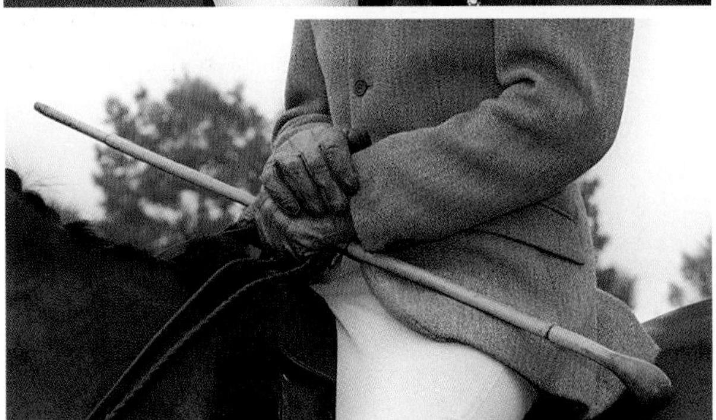

RIGHT: A typical child's outfit suitable for any class. The jacket may be tweed, navy blue, or black. Neatness is always most important.

A totally different, very neat picture from that next door! It immediately gives the impression of being professional.

BELOW: An unsuitable hairstyle which detracts from the overall picture and obliterates the number. There are also too many ribbons to look professional, even on a child.

person using it. It should not be longer than 30 ins (76 cms), except in side-saddle classes.

CLOTHES FOR THE HANDLER – IN-HAND CLASSES

As for all showing, the handler must be as neat, tidy and well-turned-out as the horse itself. Men generally wear a collar and tie with a hacking jacket, tidy trousers, and a bowler hat or cap as appropriate. Women can wear the same either with a hunting cap or headscarf. Shoes should be sensible and non-slip, and suitable for running the horse up in hand. Neat and tidy skirts are acceptable but high fashion clothes are inappropriate. A show cane should always be carried and gloves worn.

Two smart handlers wearing suitable clothing for any in-hand showing class. Note the sensible shoes, show cane and gloves. A double bridle or Pelham is suitable for horses over the age of three.

For some sport horse classes the handlers may be expected to wear 'whites' (trousers or overalls), which will be specified in the rules. The horses may need to be run up in a triangle, so good running shoes are essential.

- Some handlers wear co-ordinated outfits to accentuate the colour of their horse. If you wish to do this, take care – if overdone, it can actually detract from your horse.

Clothes for the groom

- Neatness in the ring is expected and a tidy jacket worn over a shirt and tie would be ideal. Either jodhpurs or neat slacks should be worn. A riding hat finishes off the picture. The groom is a very good indication of what sort of establishment the animal comes from.

BELOW: Traditional dress is quite common in mountain and moorland classes – it is not too difficult to recognise that this is a Highland pony!

BELOW RIGHT: An extremely smart groom who has probably already led a child in a leading-rein class and has all the necessary equipment in her basket. She is wearing sensible shoes for both leading and grooming.

ON THE DAY

Make sure your own riding kit is complete:

- Boots and spurs.
- Breeches or jodhpurs.
- Shirt, tie and/or stock and stock-pin.
- Tweed coat.
- Gloves.
- Whip or cane.
- Hunting cap, bowler or top hat as applicable.
- Some safety pins for emergencies.
- For ladies, a bun, pins, ribbons and hairnets as necessary.
- Take some spare large clothes to wear over your breeches to keep the latter clean.
- Extra footwear and wellingtons, especially if it is likely to be wet.
- Clothes brush to give a final tidy up.
- Waterproof clothing.
- Dark tape for tying on number.

Buttonholes, if worn, need to be neat and tidy and not too over-the-top. It is the horse being judged so it is important that any adornment does not detract from the overall picture.

TABLES OF RECOMMENDED DRESS

Recommended dress for ridden hunters, working hunter classes, cobs and riding horses

County shows

- Bowler hat for men; bowler or hunting cap for women. Skull caps with harness compulsory for jumping phase.
- Tweed coat for men; tweed coat or plain blue or black coat for women.
- Plain fawn or buff-coloured breeches, not white.
- Plain black or brown boots.
- Garter straps (except on dressage boots) – points must face outward.

TIP
Buttonholes or white breeches with tweed coats are incorrect. Check the turnout for the class before the show day.

A well-turned-out horse and rider showing typical dress for hacks, with the horse wearing a coloured browband. Navy blue or black jackets are always appropriate for hack classes.

- Spurs – these must be high on heel of boot and horizontal, with the buckle on the outside and shank pointing downwards.
- Any form of string or leather gloves – brown or beige.
- Plain Malacca or leather-covered cane, not exceeding 30 ins (76 cm).
- Collar and ordinary tie – tie must be pinned down.
- Ordinary shirt.

London and Royal shows, National Championship show, and evening championships

In the morning: as for county shows (above).

- Hunting dress with hunting whip, details as follows:
- Men wear a scarlet or black hunt coat, either ordinary pattern or cut-away. White breeches must be worn with scarlet coat, and boots with tops and white garter straps. White breeches must only be worn with top boots. Black patent top boots must only be worn with a black hunt coat. A top hat and hunting tie (stock) should be worn.
- Women wear a black or blue hunting coat with bowler hat or hunting cap, plus fawn breeches and black boots with garter straps. Some women now wear a top hat and hunting tie (stock) in the evening. White breeches are not favoured.
- A carnation can be worn with evening wear.

Note: For riding horse classes in the evening men wear black tail coats.

Recommended dress for hacks

County shows

- Bowler hat for men; bowler or hunting cap for women.
- Tweed coat for men; women usually wear blue or black coat.
- Plain fawn or buff-coloured breeches for men; women usually wear cream or canary.
- Plain collar and tie, with pin, and ordinary shirt.
- Spurs.
- Plain black or brown boots (wear black boots with a black or navy coat).
- Garter straps (except on dressage boots).
- String or leather gloves.
- Plain Malacca or leather-covered cane, not exceeding 30 ins (76 cm).

Evening

- Ladies wear top hat with white hunting tie (stock), plus breeches, black boots and plain or cut-away blue or black coat, gloves and cane.
- Men wear black frock coat and waistcoat, with tight-fitting black trousers (overalls), ordinary collar and tie or cravat, black jodhpur boots, gloves and cane.
- A neat buttonhole or carnation.

Recommended dress for best-trained classes for hacks, cobs and riding horses

As for London and Royal shows: above.

Recommended dress for mountain and moorland classes – adults

- Tweed coat.
- Ordinary shirt with collar and tie.
- Bowler for men; bowler or hunting cap for women. Skull cap for any jumping phases.
- Fawn or buff-coloured breeches or jodhpurs.
- Plain black or brown hunting boots or jodhpur boots.
- String or leather gloves.
- Plain Malacca or leather-covered cane.
- No spurs.

Recommended dress for side-saddle classes, including equitation

Adults – county shows

- Ordinary habit, with collar and tie. (Habits are generally blue, black or a mellow tweed. The latter is not worn at London shows nor with a top hat.)
- Bowler hat and veil.
- Plain leather or string gloves.
- Plain Malacca or leather-covered cane, or longer whip.
- One spur.

Adults – London and Royal shows

- As for county shows, or habit with hunting tie (stock); a top hat and veil may be worn in the afternoons or evenings.

Children

- Habit with collar and tie.
- Hunting cap with safety harness (conforming to current rules).
- Leather or string gloves.
- Show cane.
- No spurs.
- Neat buttonholes can be worn with blue or black coats, never with tweed.

REMEMBER
It is the pony not the child that is being judged. Too many fancy ribbons distract the eye and are unprofessional.

Recommended dress for in-hand classes

- Men should wear a suit or coat and trousers, collar and tie and a bowler hat.
- Women may wear a coat and trousers with a collar and tie or must otherwise be neatly dressed.
- Suitable shoes to run in.
- A plain or leather-covered cane should always be carried.
- Gloves should be worn.

Recommended dress for children's ridden classes

- Tweed coat or blue/black coat in leading-rein and first ridden classes. (Tweed coats are seen less and less today.)
- Blue, black or brown coats for show classes.
- Tweed coats for working hunter and show hunter pony classes.
- Blue or black hunting cap with safety harness, or crash hats with blue or black cover – compulsory for jumping.
- Cream or beige jodhpurs.
- Black or brown jodhpur boots.
- Plain shirt and a tie, often colour-coordinated.
- No spurs.
- Girls' hair should be neatly plaited, bunched or secured in a hairnet if necessary.
- Neat buttonholes can be worn with blue or black jackets, never with tweed.
- Handlers in leading-rein classes should be neatly dressed and should always wear a hat, jacket, gloves and suitable shoes.
- Show cane or whip as appropriate.

CHAPTER 7

Show Tack and Equipment

The tack that you show your horse in is very important as in some cases it can influence the looks of your horse. **Whether ridden or in hand the tack must complement the horse**, be suitable for the type of horse, be safe, secure and, above all, clean and well polished.

RIDDEN CLASSES

- The **bridle** of choice for all ridden classes is the double bridle. This is always correct in the show ring. Three- and four-year-olds, however, usually wear snaffle bridles. A pelham can be used if the horse or pony is not quite ready for the double. Pelhams with couplings are very useful in children's classes as little hands often find two reins a bit much to cope with.
- The bridle should be neat and tidy with all the keepers working properly to keep all ends in place. Decorative stitching is attractive and suitable for hacks, children's show ponies and riding horses but would be considered inappropriate for hunters, cobs, working hunters, and purebred mountain and moorlands which are unplaited. These should have strong-looking bridles relative to their size.
- Very elegant animals, such as hacks and show ponies, will generally be best in narrow leather bridles, while the hunter and working types need sensible wider leather ones.
- Whatever the bridle, make sure the **reins** are not too long. Loops of leather rein hanging down look unsightly, and children can get their

TIP
Wearing coloured browbands in working hunter, hunter, cob or mountain and moorland classes is incorrect and very unprofessional. Always check correct turnout.

Elegant bridle with coloured browband, used for hacks, riding horse and childrens' show pony classes. (The throatlash looks a little on the tight side for a ridden horse.)

feet caught up in them. Plaited leather reins are acceptable and give a little more grip; it is usual to have these on the bridoon rein of the double bridle.

- Coloured **browbands** are usual in hack, riding horse and show pony classes. These should be neat and tidily finished at the ends and not too ostentatious. They should be the correct size for the animal concerned. There are many different designs available, so choose one that complements your animal's head.
- The **noseband** can improve or detract from the look of the animal. A wide noseband and wide browband have the effect of shortening the head. A small head is not a fault but will look better with a narrow noseband and matching browband. Decorative stitching is usual on those worn by ponies, hacks and riding horses, but use a plain noseband for cobs, hunters and workers.

Stronger looking bridle with plain browband, used for hunter, cob and working hunter horse or pony classes.

1 browband
2 cheekpiece
3 cavesson noseband
4 curb cheek ring
5 curb bit
6 curb chain
7 cheek
8 lip strap
9 curb rein
10 curb hook
11 bridoon rein
12 bridoon bit
13 cheekpiece
14 throatlash or throatlatch
15 bridoon slip head
16 headpiece

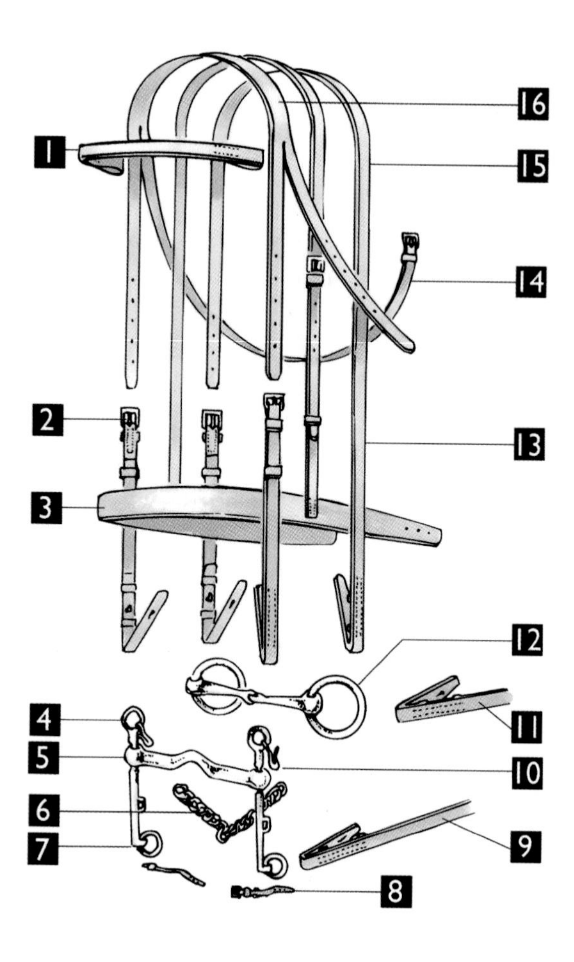

FITTING THE CURB CHAIN

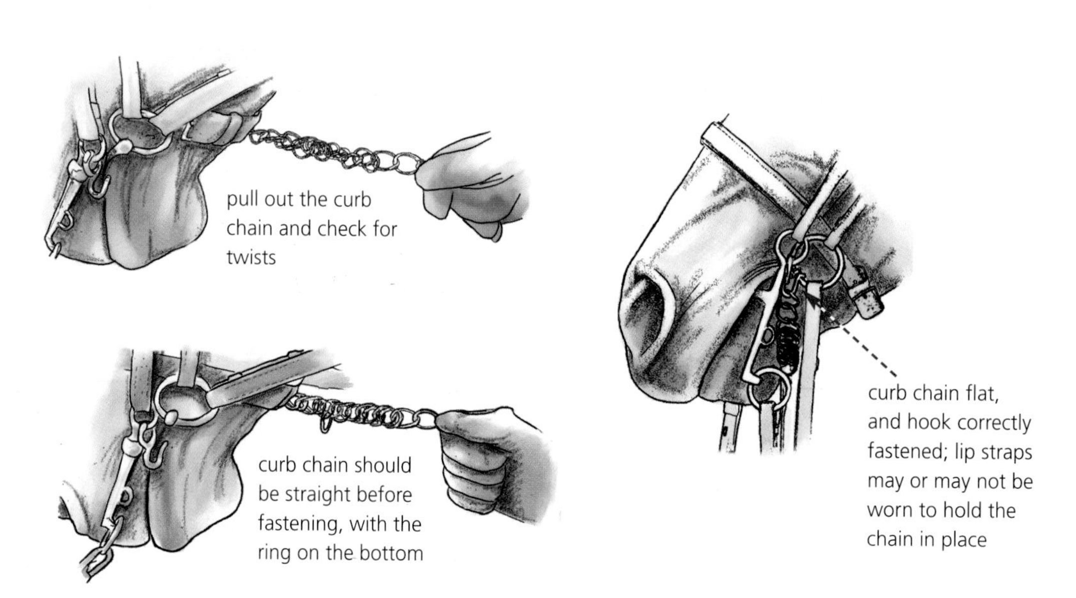

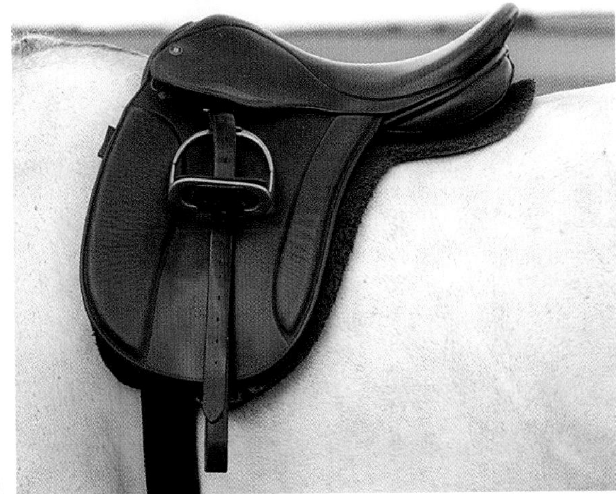

Dark numnahs on dark horses are usual. On greys, it is very important that the numnah really fits the saddle. Dark or white can work equally well but check the overall picture at home before deciding.

- **Saddles** should be carefully considered to ensure that they suit the horse's make and shape. Show saddles are cut very straight to show off the shoulder to its best advantage. A forward-cut saddle is apt to cover up the horse's front. On the show horse the saddle should be set back as far as possible and should be comfortable to sit on, especially if the judge is going to ride. Saddles and bridles should match in colour – for example, if using a black leather or synthetic saddle, a black leather bridle is appropriate.

- **Girths** should be either leather (used generally for hunters, cobs, riding horses and working hunters) or webbing (more usual for ponies and hacks). The width of the girth and size of the saddle can enhance or detract from your horse, so will the colour. Use white on greys and dark on dark colours. A small saddle with narrow girths will look fine on a short-

Two fancy browbands, for ponies, hacks or riding horse classes. If your exhibit's head is not its strong point, use a discreet browband. Ensure that ribbons cannot interfere with the eye. Trim them, if necessary.

coupled animal but may look ridiculous on a slightly longer-backed horse, so with this type use a larger saddle and a broad girth placed a little further back to 'shorten' the horse.

- If your horse is to be ridden by a judge, check that the leathers can be adjusted for any judge, tall or short, and that the stirrup irons will accommodate small or large feet. It may be necessary to keep a set just for the show ring, and these can be brought in by the groom at the appropriate time.
- Try your horse in a few different bridles and saddles and take a critical look at him so that you can see for yourself what he looks like and which seems right for his make and shape.
- **Numnahs** should not be necessary with a good well-fitted saddle, but if you must use one ensure that it is very discreet and fits the saddle profile. Pure wool ones can be cut to the exact shape of your saddle. Numnahs can match the saddle or the horse; white numnahs look fine on greys, but a black or brown one will look better with a darker animal. If used, numnahs must be spotlessly clean, especially white ones, otherwise they will detract from the overall picture.
- For leading-rein classes, a neat **lead rein** of leather or white webbing is required. It should be attached directly to the noseband only.
- For **side-saddle** classes, the saddle must fit correctly, sitting evenly and

This side-saddle appears to be sitting on a rather over-large pad, but the saddle is sitting square, which is most important.

squarely either side of the backbone. The stirrup must be adjustable to cater for different sizes of judge, and, when mounted, should allow the hand to fit in between your leg and the leaping head. This ensures that there is enough room to raise your heel up into the leaping head for extra security when necessary. The girth should be the correct length for your horse – this is worth checking carefully each year. There is nothing worse than discovering at the beginning of the season that the girth is just too short or too long and unsafe for riding. Some saddles have the girth and balance strap combined, which is easier to cope with in the show ring, but they must be the right length. The type that has a separate balance strap must be carefully checked to ensure that the strap does not get left behind. It is a wise precaution to leave one end attached to the saddle at all times.

Tip
If in doubt about show bridles, use a fairly plain one that shows your horse off to its best advantage. The judge wants to look at the animal, not at what it is wearing.

In-hand classes

To be shown in hand the horse requires a neat show bridle, leather slip or halter, depending on his age and class.

- Most youngstock are shown in a plain in-hand bridle with a rubber or mild bit and a lead rein. Some bridles have discreet metalwork, but

Two different types of halter. Never tie up animals without making a knot first, to prevent overtightening round the jaw.

Tip
Never forget to take your horse's flu vaccination certificate – many an unfortunate exhibitor has been sent home from a big show for failing to produce one when required.

or strikes into itself. Putting these on, at least until it has settled down and always when lungeing, is sensible.

4. The in-hand animal will require its in-hand bridle, and show roller and side-reins if used. A spare lead rein is worth having, just in case anything goes wrong, as are a spare headcollar and lead rope.
5. Hay and water plus a feed are essential to keep the animal happy and contented; it will help to settle a youngster if he has something to nibble at during the day.
6. Don't forget buckets and feed bins.
7. The grooming kit, with all necessary brushes, oils and plaiting equipment, 'diamond' comb or template, plus a clean brush, sponge and stable rubber to take into the ring, should be included.
8. Always have your tack-cleaning kit with you, and take boot polish for your own boots and any tack that needs buffing up. Metal polish and a duster are also a must.
9. Rugs, sheets and waterproofs should be packed to cater for unpredictable weather, plus a smart well-fitting roller or surcingle.

Not all exhibitors are quite as well prepared for the elements as this pair! It certainly helps to be ready for all weather conditions.

'I think I should win – don't you?' This neat, tidy and well-fitting bridle enhances, rather than detracts from, this youngster's head.

10. Skip and shovel with brush, plus bag to put manure in. Never tip this out on the showground, nor leave your site untidy.
11. Travelling kit (see below).
12. First-aid kit for both horse and rider, plus horse and rider essentials such as: entry numbers, horse passports, flu vaccination certificates, show details, food, drinks, mobile phones, etc.

Travelling to the Show

The travelling kit should include travel boots, plus knee and hock boots if necessary. If your horse is not a good traveller extra protection may be necessary to prevent him damaging himself. Bandaging the legs, before putting on generous travel boots which incorporate knee and hock protection, may help. A poll guard to protect the head is also wise.

The tail needs to be well protected with a bandage and tail guard. Loosely plaiting the tail and folding it up, or putting on a nylon stocking or cover to keep it clean, will save one more chore on arrival at the show.

Allow the horse as much space in the box as possible and drive very slowly, especially if the roads are twisty. Give yourself extra time for travelling with a difficult horse as so much depends on gaining his confidence, something which can never be done if you are in a hurry. Make sure the floor is not slippery; lay down straw or shavings to prevent this. Some bedding will also encourage the horse to stale, which he may be unhappy to do on a rubber or plain floor.

CHAPTER 8

Presentation

Producing the horse for the ring is an art that takes years to perfect. The plaiting, turnout, grooming, way of going and general condition of the horse or pony combine to make the overall picture that you present to the judge. Naturally you will want to attract his attention early on in the class, especially when the ring is teeming with other exhibits.

MANES AND TAILS

- Plaiting can make an enormous difference to your horse's appearance. If plaiting is new to you **practise** daily until you have perfected the art. Ask a professional to show you how to do it. Ensure that you plait tightly, then fold or roll the plait and secure well.
- A **poor neck** can be improved tremendously by pulling the plaits upwards on to the top of the neck and then rolling them up so they rest neatly and evenly on top. Larger rather than smaller plaits will be best, so do not pull the mane too short to start with. If the plaits are pulled down on this type of neck they accentuate the problem. A poor neck will not improve your showing prospects, so unless you can plait it cosmetically to improve the outline, your chances of success will not be great until the neck improves.
- **Elastic bands should never be used for showing; all plaits must be sewn in place with thread or wool of a suitable colour.**
- A horse with an **overdeveloped crest** will need its neckline fined down. The mane should therefore be well pulled, and small plaits should be

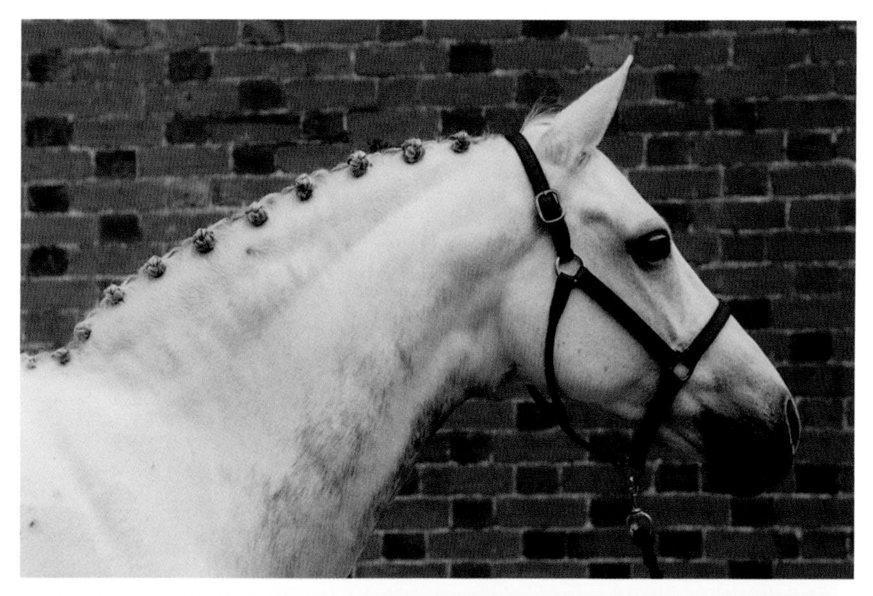

These plaits follow the line of the pony's neck. They are neat and regular and pulled down snugly into the well-muscled neck.

Untidy plaits, which do nothing for this pony. Plaits should enhance the animal's neck by their size and positioning.

rolled down on to the neck to ensure no extra prominence is given. Keep them evenly spaced.

- A **good neck** should be enhanced by beautifully neat and even plaits all the way down the neck. Remember no plaits will look really good unless the mane has been well pulled and is all the same length before you start.
- Before you set about pulling a mane be quite sure that you do not intend to show your horse or pony in classes for mountain and moor-

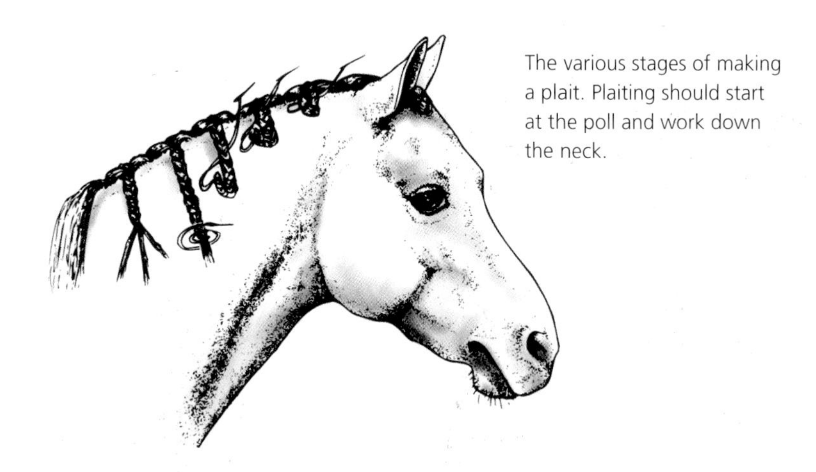
The various stages of making a plait. Plaiting should start at the poll and work down the neck.

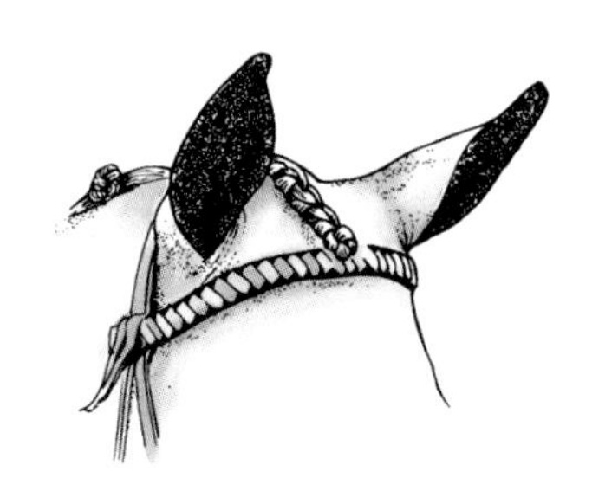
The forelock can be plaited in two ways, as shown above.Use whichever suits your animal best.

lands, palominos, pure-bred Arabs, etc., as in many of these classes manes should be left natural, although some discreet tidying is usually permitted. If you need to plait these animals for other classes it is best to have a couple of practice sessions at home to see which size plait produces the best result.

- When **hogging** manes be sure to get an even cut along both sides of the crest of the neck as well as up the middle. This is best done about three days before the show to allow the hair to grow a fraction.
- Heavy horses are normally plaited or braided with raffia or coloured wool, and plenty of practice is required to perfect the technique. Their tails are also put up or the docks clipped.

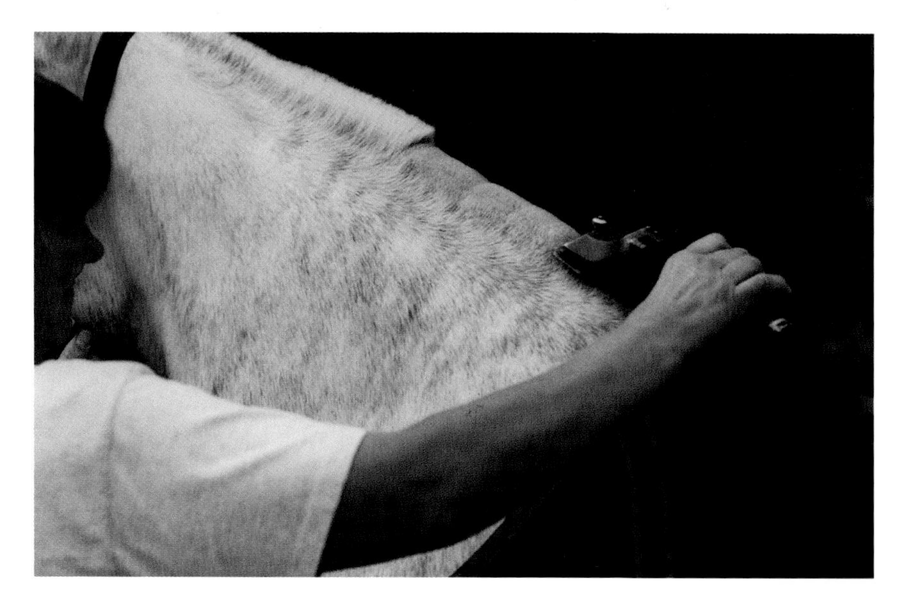
Hogging the show cob is best done a few days before the show. Ensure that it is smooth and even, checking from both sides.

This method of tail plaiting produces a flat central plait. Tightness is essential for a neat result.

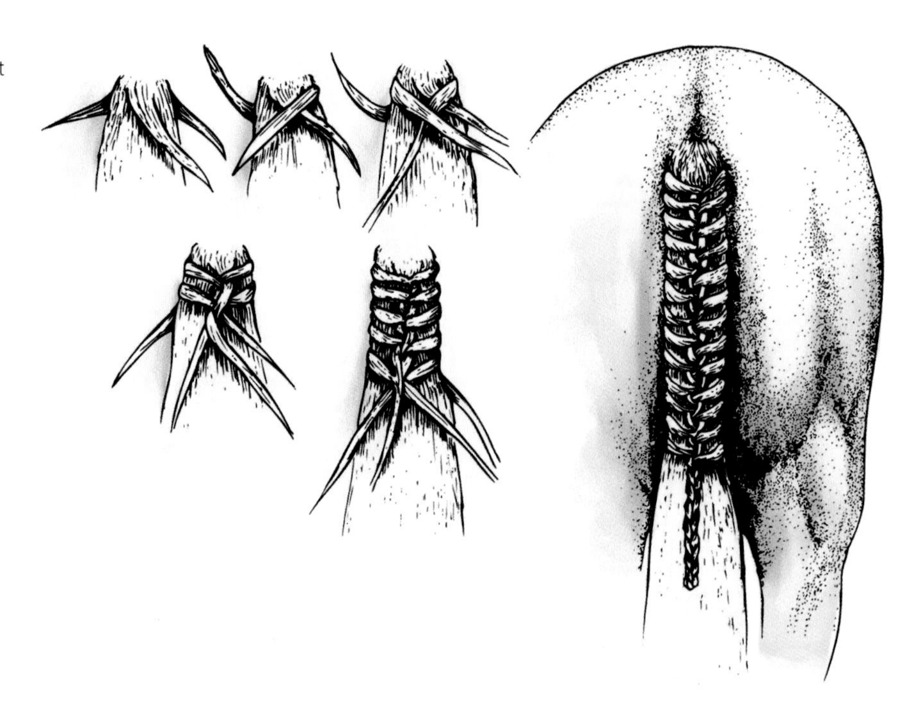

This method of tail plaiting produces a raised central plait. For good results, take in even-sized strands of hair and finish off neatly.

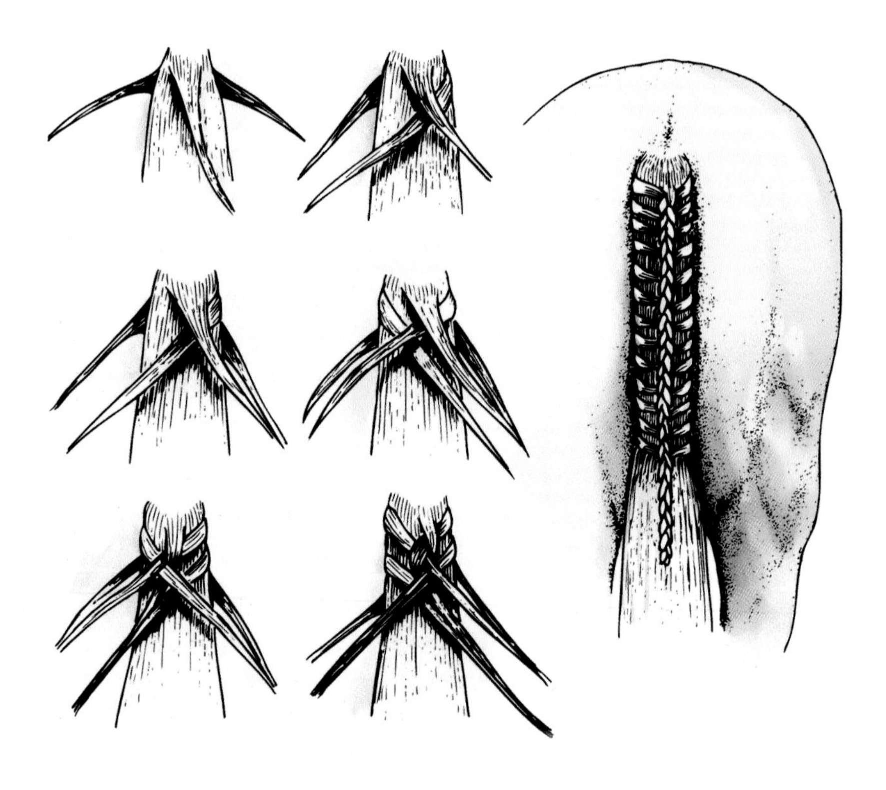

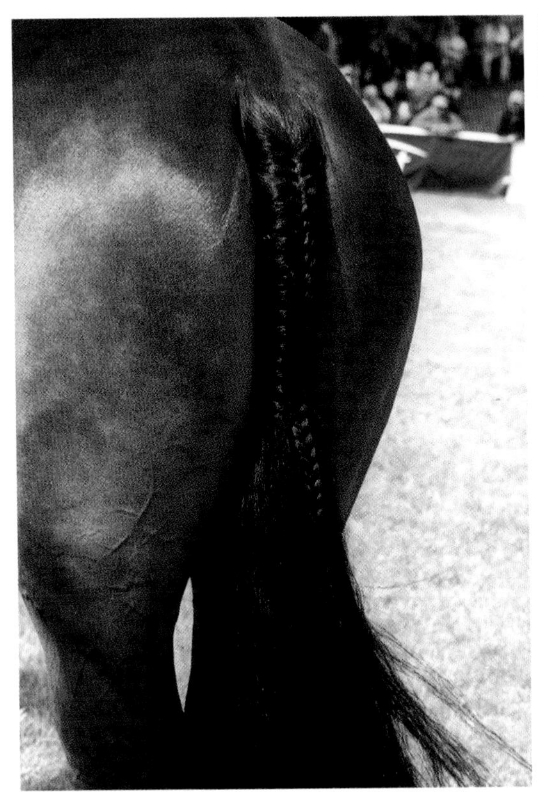

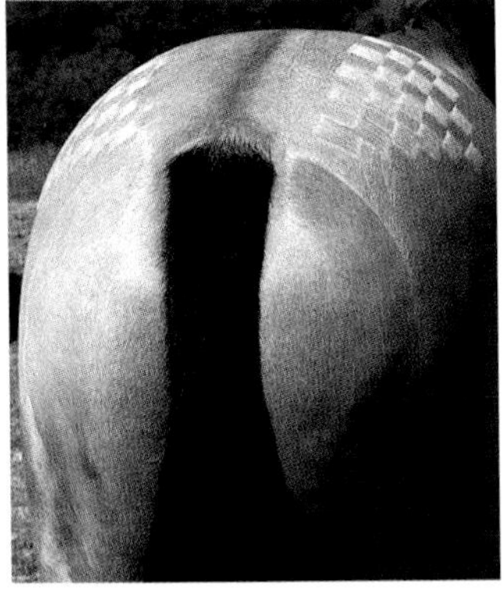

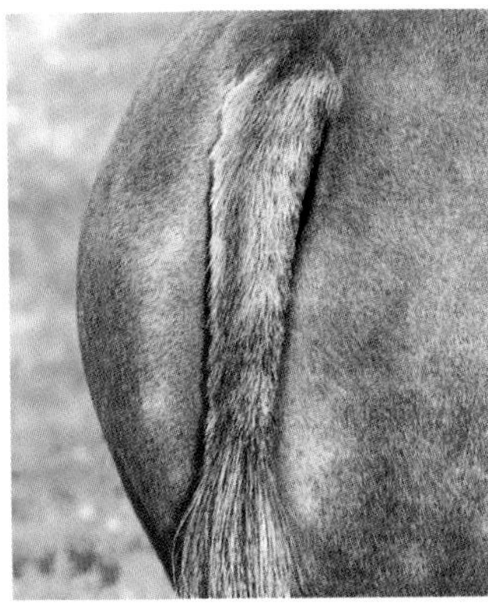

A neatly presented tail puts the finishing touches to your exhibit. The modern 'quick fix' method of clipping a tail (shown bottom right) is to be abhorred, however.

- Tail plaiting should enhance the shape of the quarters and the look of the tail. To be successful the tail hairs at the top need to be quite long, preferably never having been pulled, and the plaiting should continue down the tail just far enough to give a good line to the quarters.
- The tail plait should be neatly finished off, usually by being looped back on itself and stitched in place. Once plaited, make sure you curve the tail nicely into the shape of the quarters so that the end hangs naturally.
- If the tail is pulled this should be neat and tidy and kept well bandaged during the day so that it remains in shape.
- Once a properly pulled tail is as you require it, and it may well take a week or so to get it that way with the more sensitive horses, it only requires a few minutes a week to keep it looking good.
- The length is important and for most ridden animals 4 ins (10cm) below the point of hock is a good rough guide. Before cutting the tail, however, always study how your horse carries his tail. Some carry them high, others low, and it is this, and what will look best for your particular horse, that will be the deciding factors.

- When you cut the tail place your arm under the dock to raise it into the horse's normal carrying position, then ask an assistant to cut it straight across at the required length.
- Too long a tail can detract from the overall balance of the show horse. In Britain the 'bang' tail (i.e. one that is cut straight across) has been in vogue for years but in other countries a longer tail left natural is more usual.
- Never brush out the bottom of the tail as this causes hairs to be pulled out. There are several 'detanglers' on the market which can be sprayed on to help keep the hair tangle-free. Always hold the top of the tail firmly below the dock and only then brush out so as not to pull out hairs. Baby oil or similar can be wiped lightly over the tail to give a gloss. Wavy tails look unprofessional, so never plait up tightly when bringing your horse to a show as the wave will take some time to drop out.

TRIMMING

Trimming of the show horse is another important aspect but with many pure-bred mountain and moorland classes and heavy horses etc., feather is left natural, so don't get carried away until you are quite sure that you have decided which classes you wish to enter. Discreet tidying will be necessary, though.

- All trimming should be done discreetly, making it look as natural as possible. This is generally quite easy with the finer breeds, which tend not to carry excess hair. Ears are usually tidied up down the front and trimmed slightly inside if they tend to be too fluffy.
- A small section of mane just behind the ears should be removed to allow the bridle or headcollar to 'sit' comfortably. When clipping or trimming this area take care not to remove too wide a section – about 1½ins (3–4cm) is about right. The practice of cutting the mane right back at the poll and doing the same at the withers ruins the look of the horse and is definitely not to be encouraged.
- Whiskers are generally clipped or trimmed off the lighter types of animal, such as ponies, hacks and riding horses, but may be left on hunters, cobs, native breeds, heavy horses, etc., although very long whiskers may need a slight tidy-up. This is a matter of personal preference.
- The heels are usually trimmed for all ridden show classes and this can either be done with clippers or a comb and scissors. Care must be taken

Small hand trimmers are ideal for trimming whiskers and around the head, sometimes a sensitive area.

not to create a 'stepped' look, so trimming must be neat and even.

- Heavy breeds and mountain and moorlands with feathers are usually left natural but produced spotlessly clean and well brushed. White feather is often whitened with chalk to enhance the colour and then well brushed on the day of the show.

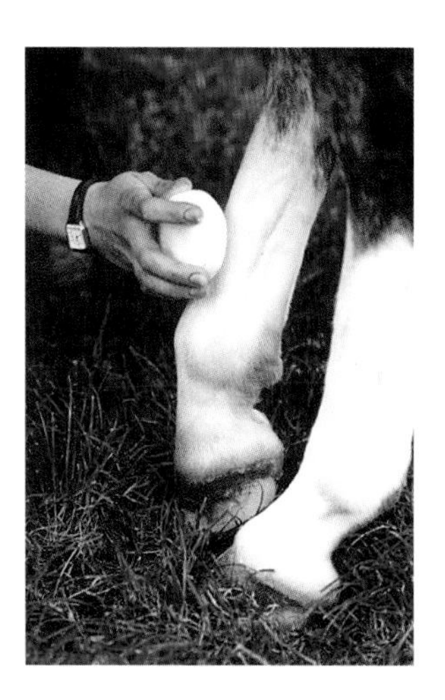

Whitening the socks with a chalk block adds a little extra sparkle to the show horse.

WASHING

- Washing of the horse is often carried out a few days before a show, or the day before if the horse is liable to sweat. It is seldom necessary to do this with all types but is advisable to wash the mane and tail before a show, also the legs from knees and hocks downwards. Be careful not to give your horse a chill if washing him all over. Wash the mane and body quickly then rug him up well before finishing off the tail and legs. A brisk walk afterwards will warm him up and ensure that he does not get cold.
- If the horse has been well groomed daily, a wash is usually only indicated if he actually looks dirty, but many people wash automatically before a show, especially in hot weather. Avoid washing too frequently as shampoo tends to remove the natural oils in the skin and can make the coat a little fluffy, especially near coat-changing time. Good, thorough grooming will ensure a clean glossy coat.

THE COAT AND CLIPPING

- Rugging of the show horse is very important if its summer coat is to stay looking good throughout the season, so keeping it warm is the very first priority. This is especially necessary if you are aiming for a big show at the end of the season, such as the Horse of the Year Show which, being in October, means that most horses are just about to or have already started to get their winter coat and lose their summer bloom. Keeping the show horse warm will help to encourage the summer coat to come through early and prevent the winter one arriving too soon.
- When to clip, if this is likely to be necessary, such as with ridden horses, is a difficult decision to make. It is most important that this is done before the summer coat starts to come through otherwise the clipping can damage the new growth. The show horse is best clipped right out so that no lines are left. A good clip should not leave any marks on the coat and should follow the direction of the coat throughout.

A beautifully presented and worthy winner. Stocks, however, are generally only worn with long boots. A neat collar and tie would have perfected the overall picture.

- If you have to clip just before a show, providing you are good at the job, do it 24–48 hours beforehand. The clipped coat will usually look its best at this time. Do not rush into clipping the show horse, however, as it does have the effect of rather deadening the colour, and few horses look as good as with their proper coat. Many beautiful bright bays turn a disappointing mouse colour on being clipped, and rich chestnuts can turn into rather anaemic-looking specimens – so if you can avoid clipping, do so. Dark browns and greys are probably the two colours which are least affected.

- **Make sure you have a newly sharpened set of blades on your clippers before starting. This is essential to produce a professional finish.** Keep the horse well covered and warm afterwards.
- In the autumn some people keep hoods on their horses to encourage the coat to stay flat and grow at the same rate. Use of an infra-red light in the stable may help to keep a summer coat and encourage it to come through quicker at the beginning of the year.
- Once your horse is clipped out make quite sure it has plenty of bedding – it will have lost one layer of natural protection so may need more cushioning to prevent it from scraping hocks and joints. This will also give extra warmth.

The feet

- Make sure shoes are secure and suitable for your class. The feet of youngstock and other animals without shoes may require a quick rasp on the day you travel to ensure that there are no rough edges. Some exhibitors polish the feet with boot polish before a show, which has the advantage of being less messy than hoof oil. Either method is excellent. Some people clean white stripes on hooves by rubbing **lightly** with sandpaper. For best cosmetic effect, the feet should be attended to just before entering the ring.

Finishing touches

- The final touches before going into the ring include **darkening the eyelids and nostrils** with a little oil or Vaseline to accentuate the quality of the head. These areas and the **dock** should be sponged first and then wiped over with a very small amount of oil without making the area sticky. Cosmetic black eye shadow can also be used.
- **Coat gloss** can be applied, especially on horses who are not naturally shiny; it will help keep the tail hair tangle-free too.
- **Hairspray** can be helpful in controlling a difficult mane that refuses to

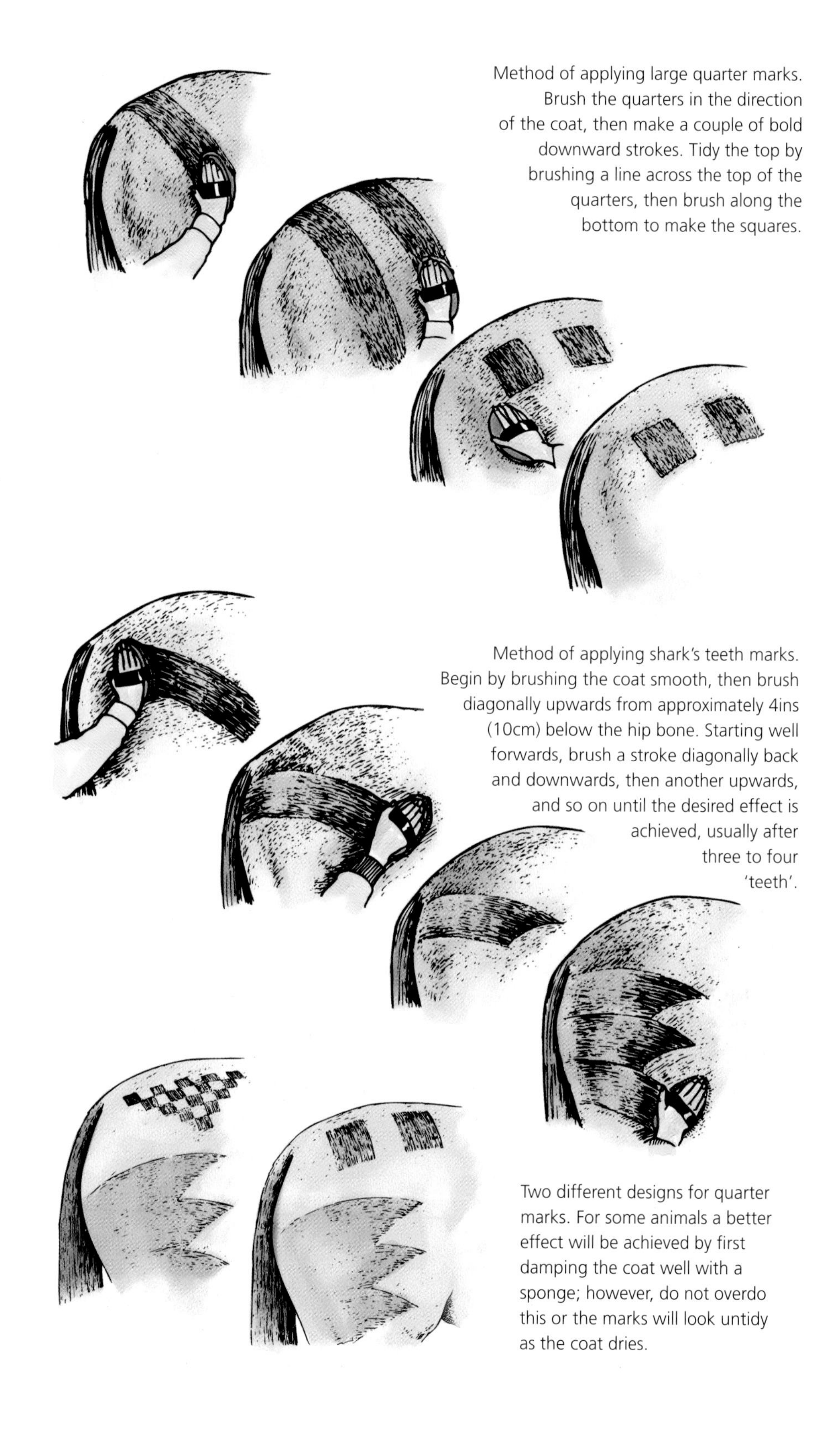

Method of applying large quarter marks. Brush the quarters in the direction of the coat, then make a couple of bold downward strokes. Tidy the top by brushing a line across the top of the quarters, then brush along the bottom to make the squares.

Method of applying shark's teeth marks. Begin by brushing the coat smooth, then brush diagonally upwards from approximately 4ins (10cm) below the hip bone. Starting well forwards, brush a stroke diagonally back and downwards, then another upwards, and so on until the desired effect is achieved, usually after three to four 'teeth'.

Two different designs for quarter marks. For some animals a better effect will be achieved by first damping the coat well with a sponge; however, do not overdo this or the marks will look untidy as the coat dries.

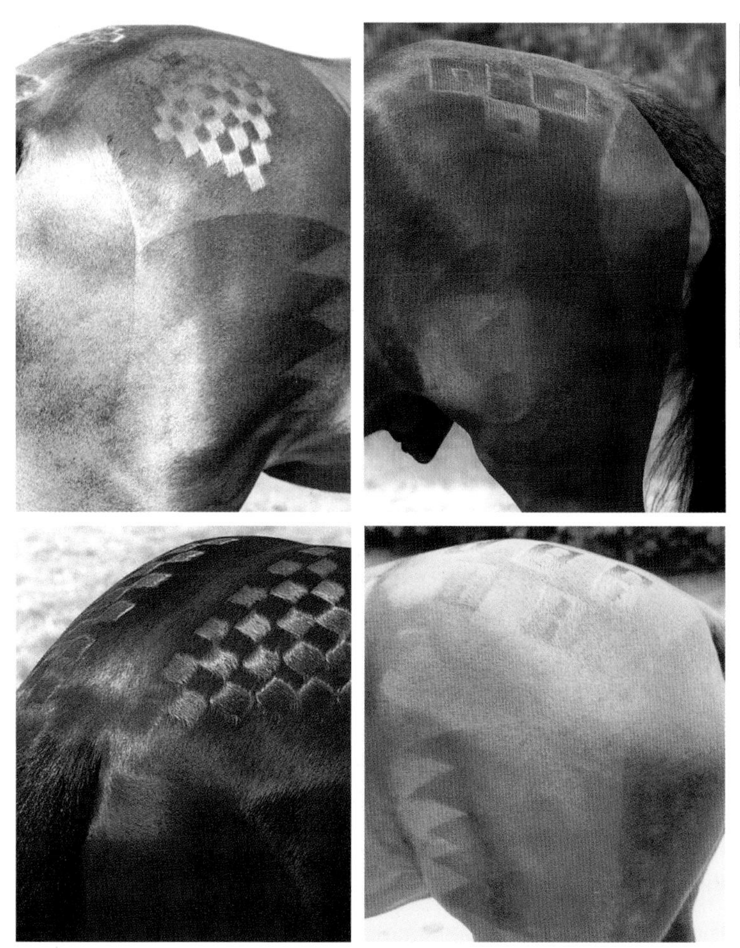

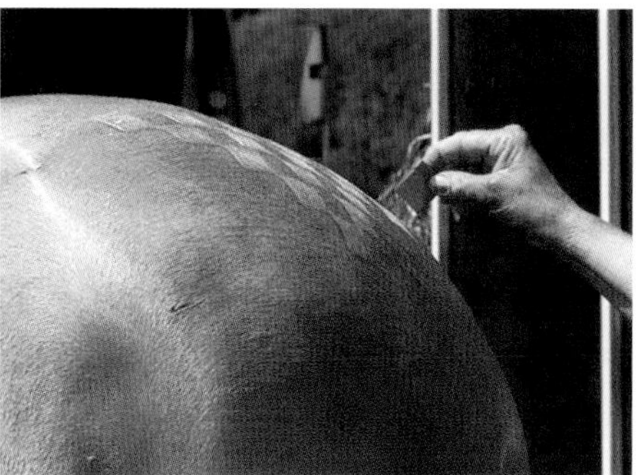

A variety of different designs to enhance the quarters. The hindquarters of the horse shown in the middle top picture, however, would be better with a small, discreet pattern so as not to draw attention to its obviously weak quarter muscles.

plait well; and can be usefully kept with the show grooming kit for emergencies to tidy up fly-away hairs.

- **Diamonds and shark's teeth** markings on the quarters are used to add a little extra elegance to the hack, child's show pony and riding horse. They are sometimes seen on hunters and may also be used in some part-bred classes. If applied they should be neat and add to the overall outlook of the animal; in no way should they detract from it or draw the eye towards a problem area.

- Diamonds can be put on with a small comb broken to about 1–1½ins long (2.5–4 cm), and with the coat brushed smoothly on the quarters, drawing it downwards in a type of chequer-board design. Alternatively templates can be made or purchased with other patterns and shapes. These are placed on the quarters and held still while the underlying hair is brushed downwards to leave the imprint. Some people use templates

The final finishing touches often make the difference between winning and losing. A little oil around the eyes, nose and dock can enhance the quality of the animal.

whose patterns are too large for their animal, which spoils the effect, so be careful to choose one that is the right size for your horse or pony. Better still, put on your own pattern.

- Shark's teeth can add interest and need practice. They should be started a little below the hip bone and put on in long sweeping strokes, making one upward stroke then one downward one, leaving a neat line of 'teeth' down the quarters. Unless these are done well they do not look good, so do practise frequently at home before attempting to do them for the show ring.

- It hardly needs to be stated that if your horse's back end is not his strong point then for goodness sake don't draw attention to it; especially with shark's teeth. These may show off your horse's inadequacies even more obviously.
- Any subtle disguising of scars or blemishes should be discreet enough so that any colouring does not come off on the judge's hand, which would be a major giveaway.
- Once you feel you have your horse more or less ready for the ring, stand back to admire your handiwork and to ensure that the overall picture is right. The tack should look clean and sparkling, the coat should be gleaming following a final dust over. Diamonds and shark's teeth, if used, should have been well applied. The tail should have been well separated by hand or lightly brushed out using spray and a soft brush; the hooves should be oiled. The plaits should have been checked, any untidy hairs sorted out and the tail bandage removed. If the mane is unplaited this should have been thoroughly brushed out, including the forelock.
- The handler (if appropriate) should be ready, looking equally neat and tidy, wearing the appropriate number trimmed, if necessary, and carrying any certificates relevant to the class.

  The rider should be neat, clean and tidy with coat well brushed and boots highly polished. Gloves, spurs and a show cane, plus the correct number, must be worn and any relevant certificates carried in the pocket.

BE PREPARED

- Make quite sure you know where the rings are, which one you are in, and the number of your class. Arrive at the collecting ring at least ten minutes before the scheduled starting time of your class. Many youngstock classes start at a set time with each class following on afterwards, so keep a constant check to ensure you don't miss yours as some of these are judged very quickly. Listen carefully for any announcements regarding your class and the day's schedule as changes do sometimes take place.
- Careful planning of the day needs to be worked out before you set off. **Allow yourself plenty of time to be able to prepare your horse looking and behaving at its best.**

A typical strong bridle and noseband on this prize-winning hunter. The top bridoon rein is generally thicker than the curb one.

- It is worth arriving early if you want to exercise, as space is often limited. Ridden horses must be well mannered; young ones in particular may require quite some time to settle down. The older horse sometimes tends to get a little ring crafty, so again may need ample work. Children's ponies often require riding or lungeing well before the child gets on, so a suitable spot should be found for lungeing if necessary. Youngsters may need a little exercise before entering the ring and if possible should be led around for a short time. These animals tend to tire quite quickly once the initial excitement wears off. Three-year-olds, however, may need a little serious work before entering the ring if they are the exuberant type.

- The best way to ensure that the animals are fairly well behaved is to give them plenty of work the day before so that they are less likely to sweat and get in a lather on the day of the show. Quiet walking after an initial trot and canter round is often the best way as it relaxes the horse and gives him a chance to settle into his surroundings. If this does not seem to be working, for goodness sake get on and give him a work-out, as good behaviour is much more important than looks.

  Many is the time I've had to ride a show horse right up to fifteen minutes before a class because it was being silly. I've then quickly washed it down, kept it walking to dry it off, and gone into the ring and won. **With showing it is most important to get your priorities right.**

However well made your horse or pony, if it is not produced in the ring according to the accepted way for that class, you are unlikely to be noticed. It is sad to see so many good horses being produced so badly, and I have often seen horses better looking than my own sitting at the bottom of the line because the owner did not know or was incapable of learning from others what was required for a particular class. It is no good moaning that the judge is no good; instead, you must set about learning what is required and ensure that by the next outing you and your show horse are produced properly.

CHAPTER 9

Tips for Exhibitors

There are certain crucial points relating to exhibiting which can make all the difference to the enjoyment of a day's showing:

1. Allow plenty of time for the journey and for preparing your animal for the ring.
2. Come well prepared for all eventualities, especially the weather; take spares in case of breakages; and plenty of food for equines and humans in case of long waits.
3. Be a good sport. Only one animal can win the class and crabbing the winner (assuming it isn't yourself!) is not going to change the result. The judge has to weigh all the pros and cons and is the only person who can see all of these. Everyone has his or her preference for a certain type, but it is the judge on the day who decides on the placings.
4. Never be rude or abusive to judges, stewards or officials. Not only is such behaviour appalling, but you could well end up being refused further entries, or worse.
5. Never be late for your class. If you are, always go straight up to the judge or steward, apologise and ask if it is permissible for you to join in. In some cases it may be, but if judging has already commenced you may have to retire gracefully, despite a 4 a.m. start or a 50-mile journey. It is your responsibility to be there on time.
6. Make quite sure you know your rules, and that your turnout and clothes are professional and suitable for the chosen class. It is embarrassing for everyone to see people doing things which are incorrect, whether done

in ignorance or not, and the offending exhibitor simply looks silly. Read the rules carefully each year, especially any new ones. All rules have been brought in for a reason and the onus is on you to know them and stick by them.

Large classes can take a long time to judge, sometimes in very hot weather. This group seem well-prepared for the wait.

7. Support your breed society or show association in every way you can to increase interest and enjoyment of that particular type of horse and class. If it is a new society or needs extra classes put on, lobby your local shows to include these in their schedules. If you can help by producing a sponsor they will usually be happy to consider it, but make quite sure you get plenty of support for any extra classes they include.

8. Above all, enjoy your day. If things go well, you will do this anyway, but that cannot happen always, so make the best of your day and look forward to the next outing, which may be more lucky for you. It would be an extremely dull world if everyone liked the same things and, while your horse may be a star to some, others will prefer a different type; you

The winner of any class is always going to be pleased! For the rest, it is important to accept your placing with good grace and be prepared to learn what you can from the experience.

will have to wait for success under another judge. Very often things go so badly wrong you can only laugh; but whatever happens, so long as you and your horse or pony have enjoyed yourselves it will always be worth doing. When the fun aspect no longer exists you may just as well give up because you will never be satisfied.

CHAPTER 10

Tips for Judges and Stewards

Judging can be an enjoyable and rewarding activity and there is always a shortage of new judges coming forward. It is hoped that would-be judges will find the following tips helpful:

1. Never arrive late for your class. To do so will cause absolute chaos; in addition, your reputation will be shattered as no one will ever rely on you again. The onus is on you to arrive and present yourself, ready to judge, at the secretary's office or designated spot at least fifteen minutes before your class is scheduled; if the show is running behind schedule, make sure the secretary knows where to find you while you wait. And always take with you the rule book relevant to the class you are judging.

2. Be consistent throughout the day. Don't put animals down for misbehaving in one class and ignore the same sort of antics in the next; and if possible stick to type.

3. Avoid obviously noticing conformational faults and blemishes. A good judge should spot curbs etc. without having to feel down the back of the hock. Some competitors love to crab and will relish the opportunity of criticising another's horse if they have seen you looking at a part of it with suspicion, whether or not it has a problem. If you must look or feel legs, do it to all the exhibits rather than pick out one or two for special scrutiny.

4. If you can't tell a horse's age (which all judges should be able to do) ask the competitor, but don't go into its breeding or other details during the class. This is particularly important with breeding classes and will quickly get you a bad name if you enquire before the classes are finished.

Judges and stewards must always be well dressed for the occasion. Judges are expected to wear hats at all affiliated shows unless otherwise stipulated. Comfortable shoes are advisable, as you are often on your feet for several hours.

5. Never look at the catalogue of entries before your class is completed. The judge should come to the class fresh, with no pre-knowledge of who or what will appear before him. Anyone seen studying details of the entries beforehand lays himself open to all sorts of criticism. It is, however, considered normal for the organisers to give you a free catalogue on completion of the judging, and it is interesting to read it afterwards. Your steward should arrange this for you.

6. Check before you start judging that your steward understands how the class is to be judged and is fully conversant with the rules for judging that particular class. If he isn't, brief him carefully, and tactfully mention to the chief steward that an experienced steward for each type of class makes everything run that much smoother for everyone, and might be more appropriate for another year.

7. Inevitably there are times when you will find yourself judging those you know quite well. Never be seen talking to friends, exhibitors, or riders before the class – this will inevitably lead to gossip. Be absolutely fair and treat everyone exactly the same in the ring.

8. Don't be influenced by seeing the big names leading or riding. It is the horse that you are judging and because it is produced by a 'pro' doesn't mean it is necessarily the best in the class. The difficulty often arises, however, when the professional makes a less good horse seem better than it really is through clever presentation, which is really what show-

Well-turned-out horse, rider and judge. Note that spurs are worn by the rider, but never by the judge.

ing is all about. It is not necessarily what you have got but how you present it that makes the difference between winning and losing.

9. Judging is a position of trust where discretion is often required. It should be remembered that anything seen in the ring is for your eyes only and should not be discussed outside.

10. Above all, don't be influenced by the opinions of others. You are there to judge the class and produce a line-up which you feel is right – unless there are two of you judging, it must be your decision on that day.

Don't penalise a horse because, for example, it behaved badly last month or appeared weak behind last year. It is the horse in front of you, on that day, in that class, that you are judging.

11. Try to stick to the timetable and judge the class as quickly as possible. If there are a lot of entries and you have a limited amount of time, work out how best to organise your judging and give everyone a good chance to be seen. This may mean seeing two shows at once or, if there are two judges, sharing the riding of the second half of the line-up. Ask your steward to ensure that the horses are ready to be run up in hand immediately when required. Children can be terribly slow about this but a good steward can soon get them organised. If you can keep up to time you will always be popular, but once you acquire a reputation for being slow, shows will be reluctant to ask you to judge.
12. Always be neat and tidy. Judges never wear spurs if riding but should carry a show cane. Comfortable shoes are a must. Ladies should wear hats in most cases for all pony and in-hand classes, so always have one with you. Go prepared for the weather.
13. Be pleasant to all, positive, fair in your decisions, and never lay yourself open to criticism. In this way you will enjoy many pleasant years of judging.

STEWARDS

A good steward is invaluable to the judge. If you are asked to steward at a show, make sure that you are conversant with the rules, are tidily dressed and have the disposition of a saint! Without these unpaid volunteers many shows would be in dire straits.

Stewards are expected to give a leg-up to the judge in classes where the judge is expected to ride. Do not accept the invitation to steward if you suffer from back trouble.

2

Guidelines and Reference Charts for Individual Classes

HUNTERS

The show hunter is expected to be strong, workmanlike, well mannered and up to the right weight for its class. It must gallop well and be a pleasure to ride for the judge. In working hunter classes a fluent clear round is expected, with a short, sharp gallop at the end of the round giving a good impression. The hunter should be shown in strong but plain tack. In four-year-old classes snaffle bridles are encouraged.

The lady's hunter should be a good hunter type but suitable for a woman to ride side-saddle. It must be a comfortable ride, well mannered and not too strong.

The three main ridden classes are for lightweight, middleweight and heavyweight hunters. There are various classes for four-year-olds, novices, juveniles (for riders between 16 and 25 years) and working hunters. The

A true champion demonstrating a good trot to an appreciative crowd.

Under the spotlight and shown off to perfection indoors.

Youngster in hand, shown in a plain bridle.

The working hunter needs to be a neat jumper and able to cope with the questions asked in the jumping phase.

latter are often divided into lightweight and heavyweight sections. 'Workers' – exceeding 15hh (153cm) – will be required to jump a course of rustic fences. In small-hunter classes the height range is 14.2hh to 15.2hh (148–158cm), and in affiliated classes a height certificate will be required for this.

In-hand classes cater for mares and foals, yearling colts and yearling, two- and three-year-old fillies and geldings. Some shows have small-hunter youngstock sections.

At affiliated shows exhibitors must be members of the Sport Horse Breeding of Great Britain, and all ridden horses registered with the appropriate section and entered on the SHB (GB) Basic Identity Record.

hibitors need not be members until their horses qualify, but must become members to compete in championships.

At certain shows there are special classes for the best-trained hack, cob or riding horse, comprising a freestyle test to music. They are designed to promote correct training and production of the show horse.

In-hand horses need not be registered, but this may be reviewed.

At affiliated shows all ridden hacks must be registered for the current year in the appropriate section and riders and exhibitors must be members of the British Show Hack, Cob and Riding Horse Association.

Hacks – Ridden

	Individual show	Diamonds & flashes	Ridden by judge	Rider age	Galloped	Coloured browband	Height certificate	Side saddle	Plaited	Double bridle or pelham
Small (exc. 148cm, not exc. 154cm) **Large** (exc. 154cm, not exc. 160cm)	✓	✓	✓	15+	a good stride out rather than gallop	✓	✓	✗	✓	✓
Novice (exc. 148cm, exc. 160cm)	✓	✓	✓	15+	as above	✓	✓	✗	✓	✓ or snaffle
Ladies	✓	✓	✓	15+	as above	✓	✓	✓	✓	✓
Championships	sometimes	✓	rarely	15+	as above	✓	✓	✗	✓	✓
Amateur owner/rider	✓	✓	✓	15+	as above	✓	✓	✗	✓	✓
Under 25	✓	✓	✓	15-24	as above	✓	✓	✗	✓	✓
Best trained	✓	✓	✗	15+	n/a	✓	✓	optional	✓	✓

Hacks – In hand

	Show	Coloured browband	Height certificate	Plaited	In-hand bridle
Broodmares – small & large	in hand	✓	✓	✓	double/pelham
Foals – to make small or large	in hand	✓	✗	optional	foal slip
Youngstock (yearlings, 2 & 3 years old)	in hand	✓	✗	✓	mild bit
Stallion – small & large	in hand	or brass	✓	✓	mild bit

NB: Novice horses competing in novice classes only need not be registered.
Tails, preferably pulled, can be plaited and are generally plaited for all youngstock classes.

Cobs

The cob is a small, chunky, weight-carrying horse. It must be beautifully mannered and a good, comfortable, easy ride – the sort of animal you would be happy to put your grandfather on. Cobs are judged like hunters and are expected to be good gallopers. Manners are essential and the whole outlook should be one of a calm but workmanlike performance.

The cob should exceed 148cm but not exceed 155cm and can be shown in lightweight or heavyweight classes, also in novice (show and working), ladies side-saddle, amateur and under-25. Lightweight cobs are those which are suitable to carry up to 14 stone and with at least $8\frac{1}{2}$ inches of bone. Heavyweights should have over 9 inches of bone and be capable of carrying 14 stone and over.

Working cobs are expected to jump at a good pace round a course of working-hunter-type jumps, and they must gallop and pull up easily.

There are now classes for best-trained hacks, cobs and riding horses at some shows, including the Royal Windsor and National Championship Show. These are mixed classes involving a freestyle test to music which in-

Top hat and tails, for championships at Royal shows in the morning.

cludes some compulsory movements.

In affiliated classes cobs must be registered and exhibitors and riders must be members of the British Show Hack, Cob and Riding Horse Association.

In 2004, experimental classes were introduced for horses of cob type over 15.1hh, to be judged as a normal cob class. Initially these horses do not need to be registered. However, as these classes evolve there will no doubt be changes, so check with the British Show Hack, Cob and Riding Horse Association for the latest information.

Cobs

	Individual show	Ridden by judge	Galloped	Boots	Plain browband	Tack	Martingale	Hogged mane	Plaited or pulled tail	Height certificate	Rider age
Lightweight and heavyweight*	✗	✓	✓	✗	✓	double bridle or pelham	✗	✓	✓	✓	15+
Novice show	✗	✓	✓	✗	✓	double/ pelham	✗	✓	✓	✓	15+
Novice working	✗	✓	✓	✓	✓	any	optional	✓	✓	✓	15+
Working	✗	✓	✓	✓	✓	any	optional	✓	✓	✓	15+
Ladies	✗	✓	✓	✗	✓	double/ pelham	✗	✓	✓	✓	15+
Under 25	✗	✓	✓	✗	✓	double/	✗	✓	✓	✓	15+
Restricted	✗	✓	✓	✗	✓	double/ pelham	✗	✓	✓	✓	15+
Amateur owner	✗	✓	✓	✗	✓	double/ pelham	✗	✓	✓	✓	15+
Maxi	✗	✓	✓	✗	✓	double/ pelham	✗	✓	✓	✓	15+

NB: Cobs do not usually have diamonds but a few discreet flashes are optional.

* Exceeding 148cm, not exceeding 155cm.

RIDING HORSES

The riding horse should have quality, substance, good bone, correct conformation, presence and true, straight action. It should be the sort of horse that falls between being a true hunter and true hack but sufficiently up to weight to carry an average adult. It should be a good well-trained ride and able to gallop. There is strong emphasis on ride and manners.

In affiliated classes exhibitors, riders and horses must be registered with the British Show Hack, Cob and Riding Horse Association. There are two height classes: exceeding 148cm but not exceeding 158cm, and exceeding 158cm; as well as classes for novices, ladies side-saddle, and under-25. Height certificates are required for horses in the smaller height section.

There are now classes for best-trained hacks, cobs and riding horses at some shows, including the Royal Windsor and National Championship Show. These are mixed classes involving a freestyle test to music which includes some compulsory movements.

LEFT: This worthy champion acknowledges the applause. Note the stock and top hat used at Royal shows for championships.

BELOW: A well-presented riding horse should be a lovely ride with good manners.

Riding horses, whether being shown indoors or outside, must be well schooled, beautifully behaved, and able to gallop.

Riding Horses – Ridden

	Show*	Ridden by judge	Galloped	Boots	Skull cap	Jumped	Coloured browband	Double bridle or pelham	Plaited	Height certificate	Rider age
Small (exc. 148cm, not exc. 158cm) **Large** (exc. 158cm)	✓	✓	✓	✗	✗	occasionally in unaffiliated	✓	✓	✓	✓ ✗	15+
Novice	✓	✓	✓	✗	✗	✗	✓	✓ †	✓	✗	15+
Ladies	✓	✓	✓	✗	✗	✗	✓	✓	✓	✗	15+
Working	✗	✓	✓	✓	✓	✓	✗	any	✓	✗	15+
Under 25	✓	✓	✓	✗	✓	✗	✓	✓	✓	✗	15–25
Restricted	✓	✓	✓	✗	✗	✗	✓	✓	✓	✗	15+
Amateur owners	✓	✓	✓	✗	✗	✗	✓	✓	✓	✗	15+

Riding Horses – In hand

		Plaited	Height certs or measured	Coloured browband	Double bridle or pelham
Stallions		✓	✗	✓	snaffle
Broodmares – small & large		✓	✗	✓	✓
Foal – to make small or large		optional	n/a	✓	foal slip
Yearling	YOUNGSTOCK	✓	✓	✓	snaffle
2-year-old	YOUNGSTOCK	✓	✓	✓	snaffle
3-year-old	YOUNGSTOCK	✓	✓	✓	snaffle

NB: Riding horses may have diamonds and flashes in all classes.

* Depending on the size of classes, judges may request a show only if time permits

† Or snaffle.

Sport Horses

Sport horses are now becoming an extremely important addition to the modern breeding industry. They generally fall into three categories as horses suitable for the Olympic disciplines of dressage, show jumping and eventing. Thoroughbreds, warmbloods and part-breds are particularly favoured. With the emphasis now being placed on bloodlines and performance, there is a recognition that certain characteristics play a major part in producing the ideal horse for a specific use. All need basically correct conformation, free, athletic movement, with a temperament and attitude to do the job expected of them. Trainability is a vital ingredient.

Emphasis on movement and paces is key to the dressage horse, as is athleticism, power and technique to the show jumper. The event horse requires stamina and courage, as well as technique and a combination of the above. Verified breeding information is increasingly a requirement to enter.

Sport horse classes are still evolving so there are a variety of formats for both ridden and in-hand classes for young horses. The most popular are for the three-, four-, five and six-year-olds. Some classes expect horses to be shown in hand and run on a triangle (see overleaf) so they can be assessed

Sport horse classes are becoming more popular. The dress is generally as for hunters, but may vary if specific to a discipline such as dressage, when blue/black jackets may be more appropriate.

from all angles. Some expect loose jumping, or lunging over fences. Some include a set dressage test followed by a course of jumps, which may include show jumps or cross-country type fences, or both, depending on the class.

It is important that the class requirements are fully understood so that the horse is well prepared beforehand. There are qualifiers and evaluations for championships, as well as stud book registrations which are becoming increasingly sought after and valuable. Check the criteria for your class with the relevant association or breed society and note what is required in the schedule on the day.

Sport Horses

	Show	Ridden by judge	Galloped	Jumped	Plain browband	Stripped
In hand	✓ triangular pattern possibly	✗	✗	✗	✓	n/a
Ridden	✓ as specified usually	✓ very occasionally	✓ as appropriate	✓ as appropriate	✓	✓

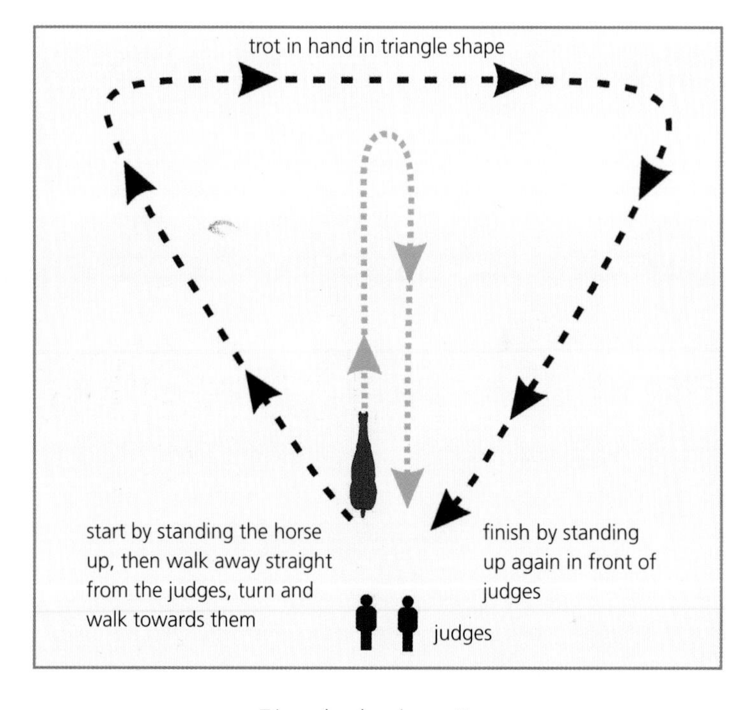

Triangular showing pattern.

SIDE-SADDLE CLASSES

The art of side-saddle riding is extremely popular. There are Side-Saddle Association equitation classes as well as working hunter, show-jumping, turnout and dressage classes. There are also the more traditional classes for ladies' hacks, cobs, riding horses, hunters, children's ponies, etc.

This ancient and extremely elegant form of riding is not particularly difficult to learn and most horses and ponies take to it readily if they are well schooled and going well on the flat. The side-saddle horse needs to have a good wither and shoulder so that the saddle sits well; the saddle must be a good fit and suit the horse.

The Side-Saddle Association is the governing body and holds its own championship show.

Side-saddle

	Individual show	Ridden by judge	Plaited	Plain browband	Stripped	Galloped	Trimmed
Equitation	✓ (test)	✗	✓	✓	✗	✗	✓
Hacks and riding horses	✓	✓	✓	✗ (coloured)	✓	✗	✓
Cobs and hunters	✗	✓	✓	✓	✓	✓	✓
Children's ponies	✓	✗	✓	✗ (coloured)	✓	✗	✓

NB: See also dress guidelines, page 66.

The position of the rider is very important in all equitation classes, as is correct turnout. Straightness in the saddle and ensuring you meet the requirements of the class are the secrets of success.

Show Ponies

Show ponies can be divided into three distinct types: the show pony, working hunter pony, and show hunter pony.

The show pony is the finest, possessing the most quality but maintaining the pony characteristics of being neat, not too wide and having an excellent temperament suitable for a child. Straight, smooth action and good general conformation with perfect manners are the essentials for all children's ponies.

The working hunter pony does not require the quality of the show pony but should possess more substance. It is required to jump a course of rustic fences according to its height.

The show hunter pony is generally expected to be a miniature version of the adult show hunter, the ideal being a mini middleweight. While not requiring the refinement of the show pony it should have plenty of quality. It is not required to jump.

There is a wide variety of classes for ponies of all sizes suitable for children of different age groups, both at novice or open standard. There are also leading rein, first ridden, side-saddle, combined training, pair and team classes. Show hunter and working hunter ponies have height classes from 122–133cm (12hh–13hh), 133–143cm (13hh–14hh) and 143–153cm (14hh–15hh). Show ponies are up to 128cm (12.2hh), exceeding 128cm (12.2hh), not exceeding 138cm (13.2hh), and exceeding 138cm (13.2hh) and not exceeding 148cm (14.2hh). There are also height restrictions for leading rein and first ridden at 122cm (12hh), and some 153cm (15hh)

BELOW and BELOW RIGHT: A future champion pony in hand, and perhaps a potential Olympic rider confidently negotiating a working-hunter-pony obstacle.

There are a mass of different pony classes to choose from relevant to the age of the rider and type, size and age of the pony. Check the rules and regulations for your particular class and its dress code.

classes, as well as intermediate classes for riders between 16 and 25 years on horses exceeding 148cm (14.2hh) but not exceeding 158cm (15.2hh).

Pony breeding and youngstock classes are also very popular, catering for all sizes, stallions, broodmares, colts and fillies.

A happy and confident picture of a well-behaved pony and determined jockey.

The British Show Pony Society is the governing body for many ridden show pony classes at affiliated shows. Some shows also affiliate to Ponies UK, which runs numerous classes and championships. At affiliated shows height certificates are required for ponies; birth certificates are required for children when applying for membership. There are winter shows and championships, which ensure year-round showing opportunities.

There are always new classes being introduced, some with qualifying shows, some without, so check each schedule carefully or ask an experienced exhibitor to explain which classes would be suitable.

Show Ponies

	Individual show	Galloped in class	Galloped in show	Stripped	Jumped	Side-saddle	Shoeing	Spurs
Show ponies	✓	according to class		✓	✗	optional	optional	✗
Show hunter ponies	✓	✓ according to class	✓	✓	✗	optional	optional	✗
Working hunter ponies/intermediates	✓	✓	✓	if time permits	✓	✗	optional	✗
Leading rein	led in hand	✗	✗	✗	✗	✗	optional	✗
First ridden	✓	✗	✗	optional	✗	✗	optional	✗
Side-saddle	✓	judge's discretion	✓	✓	✗	✓	optional	✗
Pairs	✓	✗	✓	optional	✗	optional	optional	✗
Teams/novices	✓✓	✗✗	✗✗	✓✓	✗✗	optional	optional	✗✗
Intermediates	✓	✓	✓	✓	✗	✗	✓	✗
Pony breeding classes	in hand	n/a	n/a	n/a	n/a	n/a	optional	n/a

Show Ponies – continued

	Skull cap with harness*	Snaffle bridle	Whips not to exceed 30"	4-y-o and over	Boots	Height certificate	Age limit for rider	Plaited
Show ponies	✓	any	✓	✓	✗	✓	✓	✓
Show hunter ponies	✓	any	✓	✓	✗	✓	✓	✓
Working hunter ponies/intermediates	✓ in Phase 1	any	✓	✓	✓ in Phase 1	✓	✓	✓
Leading rein	✓	✓	✓	✓	✗	✓	✓	✓
First ridden	✓	✓	✓	✓	✗	✓	✓	✓
Side-saddle	✓	any	✓	✓	✗	✓	✓	✓
Pairs	✓	any	✓	✓	✗	✓	✓	✓
Teams/novices	✓✓	any/snaffle	✓✓	✓✓	✗✗	✓✓	✓✓	✓✓
Intermediates	✓	any	✓	✓	✗	✓	✓	✓
Pony breeding classes	n/a	suitable bridle or headcollar	n/a	n/a	n/a	may be required for broodmares	n/a	n/a

* Check that skull cap and harness comply with current rules.

NB: Intermediates: for those exceeding 148cm (14.2hh) but not exceeding 15cm (15.2hh); riders under 25 on 1st June in current year. Restricted classes confined to those who have not qualified for Royal International Horse show or Horse of the Year show. Mares and geldings only eligible for BSPS classes. Youngstock will be measured on the showground. Allow time for this on arrival.

MOUNTAIN AND MOORLAND PONIES

Mountain and moorland ponies, the nine native breeds, are catered for in a wide variety of classes either as purebreds, ridden or in hand in breeds, or as mixed classes which are often split up to cater for the different heights, usually for those not exceeding 133cm (13hh) and for those exceeding 133cm (13hh). The Welsh Cob Section D has no height limit but other breeds must conform to the height limits laid down by the various breed societies.

The native ponies are all named after the regions of Britain where they have bred and run wild for years. The nine breeds are Connemara, Dales, Dartmoor, Exmoor, Fell, Highland, New Forest, Shetland and Welsh. The smaller breeds are Dartmoor, Exmoor, Shetland, Welsh Mountain Section A and Welsh Pony Section B.

The larger breeds are Dales, Fell, Connemara, New Forest, Highland, Welsh Pony (Cob type) Section C and Welsh Cob Section D.

Classes for affiliated shows, other than specific breed classes, include working hunter pony, mountain and moorland driving classes and riding pony breed and ridden classes for novices, leading rein, first ridden and in hand, etc. Some classes are restricted to junior riders only. Ponies do not need to be measured if registered with their breed society.

Plain tack and tweed jacket for this young rider in a mountain and moorland class.

At some shows classes are run for ponies other than the British native breeds, such as Haflingers, Norwegian Fjord, Icelandic, etc.

There is no age limit for riders in mountain and moorland ridden and working hunter pony classes. All ponies must be shown unplaited and only trimmed within their breed society's specifications.

The biggest championship for mountain and moorland ponies is held at the Olympia Horse Show, but most breeds hold their own breed shows.

The National Pony Society governs the overall organisation of mountain and moorland ponies. Ponies UK also run several classes and championships.

Mountain and Moorland Ponies

	Individual show	Ridden by judge	Galloped	Snaffle bridle	Coloured browbands (brass optional)	Rider any age
In hand	✓	✗	✗	✓	✗	n/a
Youngstock	✓	✗	✗	optional	✗	n/a
Working hunter pony	✓	(unusual) ✗	✓	optional	✗	✓
Driving	✓	✗	✓	optional	✗	✓
Pony breeding	✓	n/a	✓	optional	✗	n/a
Mixed M and M	✓	optional	✓	optional	✗	✓
Purebred	✓	optional	✓	optional	✗	✓
First ridden	✓	✗	✗	✓	✗	Under 12
Leading rein	✓	✗	✗	✓	✗	Under 12

	Registration required for pure-breds	Whip length	Spurs	Safety skull caps with velvet	Trimmed – only to breed specifications	Plaited manes and tails
In hand	✓	cane	✗	n/a	✗	✗
Youngstock	✓	cane	✗	n/a	✗	✗
Working hunter pony	✓	30 ins	✗	✓	✗	✗
Driving	✓	n/a	✗	n/a	✗	✗
Pony breeding	✓	cane	✗	n/a	✗	✗
Mixed M and M	✓	30 ins	✗	✓	✗	✗
Purebred	✓	30 ins	✗	✓	✗	✗
First ridden	✓	30 ins	✗	✓	✗	✗
Leading rein	✓	30 ins	✗	✓	✗	✗

NB. Height certificates are required at Olympia finals only. Ponies are not ridden in Olympia qualifiers. No make-up on ponies is allowed in mountain and moorland class. They must be shown tidy but in their natural state.

Connemara

The Connemara pony originates from the west of Ireland in the area of Connaught. This particularly bleak and tough moorland has been home to the Connemara for several centuries. The height of the Connemara varies from 13–14.2hh (133–148cm). The most dominant colour is grey but there are dun, brown, bay and black ponies, and the occasional roan or chestnut.

Connemaras are compact, deep, standing on short legs and covering a lot of ground. They have a well-balanced head and neck and free, easy, true movement. They have approximately 7–8ins of bone below the knee. Their main characteristics are their hardiness of constitution, staying power, docility, intelligence and soundness. They are particularly versatile, excelling in children's competitions and in working hunter and show hunter pony classes.

The governing body for the Connemara pony is the English Connemara Pony Society.

A typical Connemara, demonstrating natural balance on its lap of honour.

Dales

The Dales ponies are bred on the eastern hills of the Pennines. The Dales is closely related to the Fell pony, which is bred on the western side. Primarily bred as a pack pony, the Dales' main features are its placid nature, strength, energy, intelligence and very good trot. Dales are generally black or brown in colour.

The Dales pony should have a neat pony-like head, with ears that curve inwards slightly. The neck should be long and strong, the shoulders sloping and the withers fine. The hindquarters should be deep, lengthy and powerful, and the leg should have good bone measuring up to 9ins. The height of the Dales pony varies from 13.2–14.2hh (138–148cm). The Dales is distinguished by great flexion of the joints, which produces a high knee and hock action.

The Dales are used as all-round utility ponies capable of jumping and trekking. They are very popular for harness work.

The Dales Pony Society is the governing body for Dales.

A well-schooled Dales, showing itself off well during show time.

Dartmoor Pony

The Dartmoor pony breeds and runs wild on Dartmoor, Devon. It is known for its intelligence and kind, reliable temperament. The maximum height is 12.2hh (128cm) and bay, brown, black and grey are the most common colours, with roans and chestnuts occasionally being found. Skewbalds and piebalds are not allowed.

The Dartmoor is a sturdy pony with particularly good conformation. It has a neat, elegant head with small, alert ears. The neck is strong but not too heavy. The loins and hindquarters are strong and muscular. The limbs have a medium amount of bone. The pony moves with free, low strides that make it a particularly comfortable ride and an ideal child's first pony.

The Dartmoor Pony Society is the governing body.

A Dartmoor stallion demonstrating both quality and the sturdy nature of these ideal children's first ponies.

Exmoor Pony

The Exmoor pony originates from Exmoor and is claimed to be the oldest of Britain's native ponies. The Exmoors that remained in the West Country have not been crossbred and are consequently a remarkably pure breed. The Exmoor rarely exceeds 12.3hh (129.5cm) and is bay, brown or dun with mealy marking on the muzzle round the eyes and inside the flanks. There are no visible white markings. It is the only native breed to be branded, and it may not be clipped for showing.

The Exmoor is typically 'pony' with particularly short thick ears. The neck is fairly long, the chest is deep and wide and the back is broad and level as far as the loins. The legs are short and well apart. The Exmoor has a very thick coat in the winter to help insulate it against the cold; the summer coat is hard and bright. The Exmoor moves well and quite low to the ground.

The Exmoor Pony Society is the governing body.

Note the distinctive mealy eyes and muzzle of the ancient Exmoor breed.

FELL PONY

The Fell pony is closely related to the Dales pony but is generally smaller. It originates from the western side of the Pennine hills. Its height should not exceed 14hh (143cm) and it is usually black, brown or grey in colour, although a little amount of white is allowed.

The Fell is a very docile, tough, hardy, eye-catching pony with a great deal of strength. Fell ponies have a longish neck with a pony head. The quarters are muscular and strong, and the breed has good bone and strong limbs. Fells are renowned for their energetic action, which is free and straight, and for possessing their characteristic blue horn.

The Fell Pony Society, the governing body, was formed in 1912 and has helped to ensure the continuance of the breed. Fells are used for trekking, driving, and trail riding and as all-round utility ponies.

ABOVE: This Fell stallion's head captures the pony characteristics of this hardy and eye-catching breed.

RIGHT: Like many of the mountain and moorland breeds Fells are often unshod, or have only front shoes. Note the abundance of feather.

Highland Pony

This hardy pony breed originates from the Highlands in Scotland and has been part of the history there for centuries. Their height varies from 13–14.2hh (133–148cm) and the typical colours are various shades of dun, grey, brown or black, with the occasional bay and liver chestnut being seen. Most have a dorsal eel stripe running down the backbone and many have stripy markings inside the forelegs.

Highland ponies are particularly tough and this enables them to live outside all year round. They are intelligent, very strong – being quite capable of carrying weights of up to 20 stone – docile and sure-footed, and one of the most versatile of the native ponies. Today many Highland ponies are shown under saddle and are put to use carrying tourists across the steep terrain of the Scottish Highlands.

They are still used as work ponies in Scottish forests and are employed in stag hunting. Highlands have a strong neck and a wide but fairly short head. The back is compact and deep and the quarters are powerful. The legs are short, strong and with good-shaped hooves. There is a little silky feather on the legs and manes and tails are profuse.

The Highland Pony Society is the governing body.

The tough but versatile Highland pony is often grey or dun in colour.

New Forest Pony

The New Forest pony originates from the New Forest in Hampshire where it runs wild and breeds. It has the greatest height variance of the mountain and moorland breeds. Throughout the years many different breeds – Arabs, Thoroughbreds, etc. – have been let loose in the Forest to improve the breed.

The New Forest is a mixture of the strength, agility and intelligence of the native British pony but is of a narrower frame. It is a very versatile and excellent performance pony.

Its maximum height is 14.2hh (148cm) and few ponies are found to be under 12hh (122cm). Bay and brown ponies are most usual but all colours are acceptable, except piebald, skewbald or blue-eyed cream. Light chestnuts with light manes and tails may not be registered as stallions.

Forest-bred ponies are always shown in white rope halters, even the stallions, and there are classes specially for them at the breed show held in the Forest annually. Ponies off the Forest must not be trimmed at all for their classes. Others may be tidied.

This riding type of pony has substance, with a pony-type head, sloping shoulder, a deep body, strong quarters, good bone and straight legs. The 'Forester' is ideal for children and can be ridden by adults in all spheres.

The New Forest Pony and Cattle Breeding Society is the governing body.

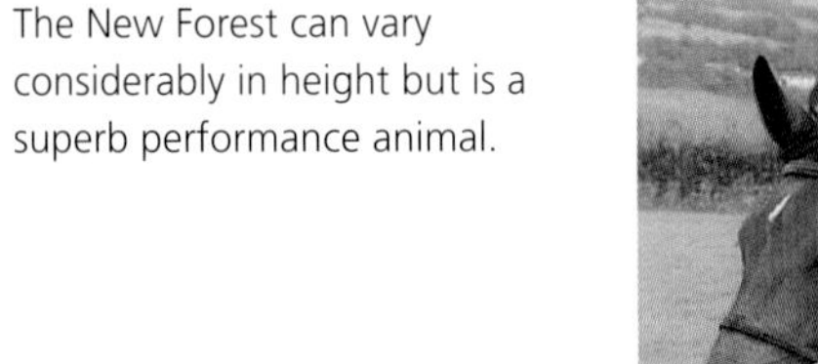

The New Forest can vary considerably in height but is a superb performance animal.

SHETLAND PONY

This pony originates from the Shetland Islands. It is the smallest British mountain and moorland pony, measuring not more than 42ins (107cm). The ponies may be bay, brown, chestnut, grey or part-colours but black is the foundation colour. The Shetland is incredibly strong relative to its size, therefore it excels in harness work; as a pack pony it is able to carry more weight in proportion to its size than any other pony or horse in the world. It also possesses great natural presence.

The Shetland's head has a broad forehead with a straight face. The neck is slightly crested and of a good length. The shoulder is sloping and the body deep. The Shetland pony grows two layers of coat in the winter, which is a particularly unusual feature, and its breed society allows clipping during the winter.

The Shetland was the first British native pony to have its own breed society, which was started in 1890. The Shetland Pony Stud Book Society is the governing body.

The smallest of the British native ponies, the Shetland is incredibly strong for its size, enabling it to carry remarkably heavy loads.

Welsh Ponies

The Welsh ponies are perhaps Britain's most beautiful native pony. Coming from the Welsh hills they are strong and tough but renowned for their exquisite heads and floating action. They have good temperaments but also have plenty of dash and jumping ability and make excellent children's ponies for all ages and sizes.

The stud book has been divided into four sections to cater for the different heights and type of pony, which are now classified as separate breeds:

Section A Welsh Mountain Ponies (not exceeding 122cm/12hh)

Section B Welsh Ponies (not exceeding 138cm/13.2hh)

Section C Welsh Ponies – cob type (not exceeding 138cm/13.2hh)

Section D Welsh Cobs

Section E for geldings is a relatively new category.

In working hunter pony classes Section Ds have to be 148cm/14.2hh or under. In all Welsh classes a long thin plait just behind the ear is the normal form of presentation.

The Welsh Pony and Cob Society is the governing body for all Welsh ponies.

Very versatile and eye-catching, the largest (Section D) and the smallest (Section A) of the Welsh pony breeds.

The four Welsh breeds are typified by these three pictures.

ABOVE LEFT: The lighter Section B. The smallest Welsh pony, the Section A (see facing page), is a miniature version of the Section B.

ABOVE RIGHT: The heavier, small cob type – Section C.

LEFT: The larger cob type – Section D.

Arab Horses

The Arab is an ancient breed with a distinctive appearance, and as with all breeds, its type and conformation are important.

The head should be small and wedge-shaped, broad at the cheek bones and relatively short. The forehead should be wide between the eyes and fairly flat. The eyes should be large and shaped like a blunted oval with wide, finely edged nostrils. Ears should be small, set wide apart and quick and alert. The neck should be long and well curved; it is carried rather higher and more proudly than in most breeds.

The chest should be wide and deep, with the loins short and strong. The back is short and level. The body is well rounded and the quarters long from the hip to the point of buttocks.

The tail carriage is one of the most distinguishing features of the breed. It should be set level with the back and carried high. Manes and tails should be free, flowing and silky.

There are classes for pure-breds, part-breds and Anglo-Arabs, both ridden and in hand. Ridden Arabs are treated as any other riding horse. There are sometimes novice as well as side-saddle classes and in-hand classes cater for stallions, broodmares and youngstock.

Manners and presentation are very important. Bridles should be discreet and strong enough to control the horse. Handlers should either wear in-

A beautiful in-hand Arabian, showing all the fine qualities of this pure and ancient breed.

The ridden Arab is usually ridden by the judge, as well as being asked to give an individual show.

Many highly successful show and competition horses are part-bred Arabs. A well-presented youngster, plaited up, unlike the purebred above.

hand dress, national dress or 'whites' with appropriate footwear. ('Whites' only for ECAHO classes.)

At affiliated shows horses, riders and owners must be registered with and members of the Arab Horse Society.

Some shows are also affiliated to the European Committee for the Arab Horse Organisation, with classes judged by a panel marking by points. Details can be obtained through the AHS.

Ridden Anglo-Arabs, plaited and treated as part-breds, compete as a general riding horse.

Foals are shown in traditional Arab style and unclipped. All colts two years and over must be bitted.

Arab – Ridden

	Individual show or pattern	Ridden by judge	Plaited	English show tack	Stripped	Galloped	Trimmed
Purebred ridden	optional	✓	✗	✓	✓	✓	✓
Anglo & part-bred	optional	✓	✓	✓	✓	✓	✓
Novice	optional	✓	✗	✓	✓	optional	✗
Western	✓	✗	✗	Western	✗	✗	✗

Arab – In hand

	Individual show or pattern	Ridden by judge	Plaited	English show tack	Stripped	Galloped	Trimmed
Purebred	✗	n/a	✗	Arab style	n/a	n/a	✗
Anglo & part-bred	✗	n/a	✓	in hand	n/a	n/a	✓
Stallions	✗	n/a	✗	Arab style	n/a	n/a	✗
Colts and fillies, 1, 2 & 3yo	✗	n/a	✗	Arab style	n/a	n/a	✗
Mares	✗	n/a	✗	Arab style	n/a	n/a	✗
Foals	✗	n/a	✗	halter	n/a	n/a	as rules

NB: Under AHS rules foals must be shown in their natural state, unclipped. All colts 2 years old and over must be bitted.

HACKNEYS

Originally a saddle horse, the Hackney was developed from trotting horses around East Anglia and Yorkshire during the eighteenth and nineteenth centuries. Hackneys are renowned for their distinctive high-stepping action and are now almost exclusively used for driving, for which sport they have become extremely popular worldwide.

The Hackney horse may be any height from 14hh/143cm (approx.) to well over 16hh/163cm, while the Hackney pony is any height up to 14hh/143cm and is virtually a breed of its own.

The shoulder and knee action is free and high and the foreleg is thrown well forward with a slight pause to give the unique Hackney movement. This is partly inherited and partly taught through the use of heavy shoes and special training. The hind action is also exaggerated.

Usually bay, dark brown or black with the occasional chestnut, Hackneys are compact, with short legs and strong hocks, and a fine but small head carried high on an arched neck.

There are in-hand classes as well as specialist Hackney classes, also all types of driving classes, including combined driving and marathons.

The Hackney Horse Society is the governing body. There is now a part-bred register.

The typical high-stepping action of the Hackney is clearly demonstrated in this elegant turnout.

Hackneys – In hand

	Height certificates	Trot or jog	Cantering	Males 'top rein' tack	Stand up cruppers	Plaited and knotted with cord	Tails loose	Nicking or docking
1, 2, 3 year olds	✗	✓	✗	optional	optional	✓	✓	✗
4 years and over	occ.	✓	✗	optional	optional	✓	✓	✗
Driven	occ.	✓	✗	✗	✗	✓	✓	✗
Stallions	occ.	✓	✗	✓	optional	✓	✓	✗

Hackneys – Driven

	Height certificates	Trot or jog	Cantering	Males 'top rein' tack	Stand up cruppers	Plaited and knotted with cord	Tails loose	Nicking or docking
Amateur	n/a	✓	✗	optional	✓	✓	✓	✗
Novice	n/a	✓	✗	optional	✓	✓	✓	✗
Open	n/a	✓	✗	optional	✓	✓	✓	✗
Single	n/a	✓	✗	optional	✓	✓	✓	✗
Pair	n/a	✓	✗	optional	✓	✓	✓	✗
Tandem	n/a	✓	✗	optional	✓	✓	✓	✗
Private driving	n/a	✓	✗	optional	✓	✓	✓	✗

NB: Ponies' and horses' height is divided at 14hh. At the National championship, Northern and Royal International Horse Shows these are subdivided into classes for 12hh and under, 12–14hh, horses 14–15hh, and over 15hh. hackneys also perform in FEI driving events under FEI rules.

WARMBLOODS

There are several different strains of warmblood horse which have evolved from crossing the Thoroughbred with the cold-blooded breeds of Europe to produce a useful performance horse suitable for today's highly competitive activities.

Each different breed that has been used has its own particular attributes and when crossed with the Thoroughbred has produced a particularly successful 'marriage'. A tractable temperament is one of the main characteristics which has made these horses so successful for dressage, show jumping and driving; and recent refinement has ensured their suitability for eventing. Classes for sport horses (see page 113) are becoming more common.

Warmblood breeding has been well established on the Continent for some time but the setting up of the British Warmblood Society has been a relatively recent innovation over here. There are strict grading rules for registration papers for all warmbloods and they are shown in hand, under saddle and judged on performance.

The main governing bodies which at present cater for warmbloods are the British Warmblood Society, the Trakehner Breeders' Fraternity, the British Hanoverian Horse Society, the British Sport Horse Register, the British Bavarian Warmblood Association, and the Anglo-European Studbook.

Warmbloods

	Continental in hand	Registration papers	Trimmed	Plaited	Plain browband	Snaffle Bridle
Broodmare	✓	✓	✓	✓	✓	✓
Colts and fillies	✓	✓	✓	optional	✓	✓
Youngstock	✓	✓	✓	✓	✓	✓
Mare grading	✓	✓	✓	✓	✓	✓
Stallion progeny	✓	✓	✓	✓	✓	✓
Sport horse †	✓	✓	✓	✓	✓	✓

NB: For most classes handlers should wear a white coat, or white shirt and trousers, but do check specific guidelines. Ensure that you know how to run the horse up in hand for your section. Some classes require a triangular pattern (see page 114) or other special presentation.

† Sport horses are eligible for grading on performance in the BWBS.

Movement and jumping ability have been carefully bred into warmbloods over generations.

Coloured Horses

Skewbald and piebald horses and ponies are generally types rather than breeds. There are a few exceptions, though, such as coloured horses/ponies belonging to Shetland, Icelandic and some Continental breeds. Shows put on classes for in hand, ridden, and best colour/markings. The animals are judged on conformation, colour and markings, and, where appropriate, on ride, performance and manners. Conformation takes precedence, with strong emphasis being placed on ride, manners and training. Continental/foreign breeds and types as well as thoroughbred/part-bred crosses are also catered for with a minimum breeding standard of 25 per cent which requires registration papers.

There are also classes for different types, such as riding horses and ponies, cobs, hunters, vanners and large British breeds.

Piebald, i.e. black and white, or skewbald, i.e. any other colour or colours and white, are the acceptable colours. The overall distribution and evenness of colour, patterns and markings as well as the depth of colour and tone are important. Patches, but not spots, play an important part.

The British Skewbald and Piebald Association (BSPA) and the Coloured Horse and Pony Society (CHAPS UK) are responsible for coloured horses and ponies.

The popularity of the coloured horse has dramatically increased in recent years, with huge classes in all sections.

This spectacular coloured horse demonstrates good colouring patterns, as well as movement.

Coloured Horses

	Individual show	Ridden by judge*	Plaited	Plain browband*	Stripped	Galloped	Trimmed (except vanners)
Ridden	✓	✓	✓ (usually)	✓	✓	✓	✓
In hand	✓	n/a	optional	✓	n/a	n/a	✓

NB: Most classes are judged according to type. Some open classes are open to all sze and types. They are generally judged as riding horse classes, except vanners (the heavier breeds).

* According to class.

PALOMINOS

The term 'palomino' refers to a colour and not to a breed. Palominos, therefore, may be found among many types of horse or pony, with colour being the main priority after correct conformation.

There are in-hand classes for all age groups as well as ridden classes, and these are judged in the usual way. The judge may ride exhibits and ask to see them galloped.

Palominos must not be plaited as the colour of their manes and tails is taken into serious consideration. There should not be more than 25% dark hairs and the coat should be the colour of a newly minted gold coin. Coats that are too dark or a wishy-washy colour will be penalised.

The British Palomino Society is the governing body.

Palominos

	Individual show	Ridden	Plaited	Hogged	Tidying of mane	Galloped	Clipped
Ridden	✓	✓	✗	✗	✓	optional	✗
In hand	✓	n/a	✗	✗	discreet	n/a	✗

Always a popular class – the golden colouring of the Palomino is enhanced by its white mane and tail.

British Spotted Ponies

This fairly rare but popular pony has existed in Britain for centuries. Although there are few rules for judging, good basic conformation is vitally important and two different types exist: (a) riding type; and (b) driving type, including cobs. They may be of any size up to and including 14.2hh (148cm).

Colouring may be leopard, snowflake or blanket. Some young animals in particular have a pronounced roan colour which does not debar them, but a more boldly marked colour is preferred. Typical characteristics are white sclera round the eye, hooves yellowish white with vertical stripes and mottled flesh marks on the bare skin. Most ponies are shown in their natural state but with trimmed facial hair, and are usually ridden by the judge. Coloured browbands are best avoided as they detract from the colouring of the animal. No cosmetic make-up is allowed.

The British Spotted Pony Society maintains a register for stallions, mares and geldings of known breeding. The Spotted Pony Breed Society of Great Britain runs affiliated classes and performance shows. They are judged on conformation, temperament and colour.

British Spotted Ponies

	Individual show	Ridden by judge	Plaited	Plain browband	Stripped	Galloped
Ridden	✓	✗	optional	✓	✓	✗
In hand	n/a	n/a	optional	✓	n/a	n/a
Driven	✓	n/a	optional	optional	n/a	✗

As with the coloureds, spotted ponies are becoming increasingly fashionable and will, undoubtedly, be seen more regularly in the show ring.

APPALOOSAS

The distinctive Appaloosa has spread from America and now boasts the third largest number of breed registrations in the world. The spotted appearance of the coat must also include a mottled skin and a white sclera round the eye. They often possess thin, wispy manes and tails, and have striped feet. There are five main coat patterns: leopard spotted, blanket spotted, snowflake, frost and marble.

Appaloosas are used for numerous purposes being strong, agile and hardy. In Britain and Europe they tend to be more of a hunter type, while in America and Australia they are more akin to a Quarter horse. In Britain they are shown in hand, and in ridden classes as general riding horses or in Western style. Because of their sparse manes they may be shown hogged or as best suits the horse. They also have their own show jumping and dressage classes run under BSJA and BHS rules.

The British Appaloosa Society is the governing body.

Appaloosas

	Stripped	Ridden by judge	Galloped	Western tack and dress	Show or pattern	Coloured browband	Plaited	Side-reins or rollers
In hand	✓	n/a	n/a	n/a	✓	✗	optional	✗
Stallions	✓	✓	✓	✗	✓	✗	optional	✗
Ridden	✓	✓	✓	✗	✓	✗	optional	n/a
Working hunter	✓	✓	✓	✗	✓	✗	optional	n/a
Riding horse	✓	✓	✓	✗	✓	✗	optional	n/a
Side-saddle	✓	optional	✓	✗	✓	✗	optional	n/a
Western	✗	✗	✓	✓	✓	✗	✗	n/a

Another very popular and versatile breed, where coat pattern causes great interest.

The Iberian Breeds

Lusitanos, Spanish Horses and Lipizzaners

	Ridden	Show	Ridden by judge	Plaited	Dress	Tack	Coloured browband
Ridden	✓	✓	optional	✗	English	snaffle	✗
In hand (1,2 & 3 years)	✗	✓	n/a	✗	n/a	show	✗
Side-saddle	✓	✓	optional	✗	traditional or English	snaffle or double	✗
Performance shows	✓	✓	optional	✗	traditional or English	traditional or English	✗
Driven	✗	✓	n/a	✗	n/a	as class	✗

occasionally a running plait

The Lusitano

The Lusitano from Portugal is a relative of the Lipizzaner, both being founded from Andalusian stock. A small, strong athletic horse with high, rounded movement, it has a wonderful temperament and was very popular with rejoneadors (bull-fighters) and for high-school movements. It is usually grey but may be any other solid colour and stands around 15–16hh (154–163cm).

The Lusitano Breed Society is the governing body.

The Lusitano, whose rider is in traditional dress, is a popular riding horse and is often shown together with the Andalusian and Lipizzaner in ridden classes.

The Spanish Horse

Formerly known in Britain as the Andalusian, the Spanish Horse hails from the Andalusian region of Spain and is shown mainly in its own breed classes. There are in-hand and ridden classes and the horses are shown with their long manes free flowing. There are two ridden classes: one is conducted in the standard way with competitors in conventional English dress and judged as a riding horse class. The other, a freestyle performance class, is ridden in Spanish dress and tack as used during fiestas. The riders give a three-minute freestyle display, which is judged 50 per cent on technical merit and 50 per cent on artistic impression.

Spanish Horses are fairly high-stepping horses but must also have reach. Dishing is not a fault in the breed neither are slight cow-hocks, although this should not be excessive.

The British Association for the Purebred Spanish Horse is the governing body for the Spanish Horse in Great Britain.

The spectacular mane of the Spanish horse makes for a fine sight when produced for the show ring or traditional fiestas.

THE LIPIZZANER

This famous breed, so well known for its displays at the Spanish Riding School and worldwide, was originally started by Archduke Charles of Austria from imported Andalusian stock, and the original stud at Lipica was set up. Usually grey in colour they may also be bay and are often born dark but lighten as they grow older. Extremely athletic, strong and intelligent with an excellent temperament, they excel at dressage and high-school work as well as carriage driving.

Apart from in purebred classes, Lipizzaners, Lusitanos and Andalusians are often shown together in ridden classes.

The Lipizzaner Society of Great Britain is the governing body.

Lipizzaners make very popular riding horses and are presented for the show ring according to the rules of the class. Purebreds are not plaited for breed classes.

HAFLINGERS

This versatile, all-round, small horse is a native of the Austrian Alps and over the years has become popular in Britain both for riding and driving. Originally the breed was very sturdy and thick-set but nowadays a taller, finer horse is preferred.

Characteristics of the breed include the chestnut colouring and flaxen mane and tail, which is strictly adhered to. White stars, blazes or stripes are acceptable, but white on the limbs or body is discouraged.

The head should be small with a slight dish and large, dark, kindly eyes. The neck should be strong and well positioned but not short; the body should be broad and deep with a strong back and well-carried tail. Limbs should be clean and hard with healthy hooves. Strong forearms and a good second thigh with short cannons are favoured. Mares usually have between $6\frac{3}{4}$–$7\frac{3}{4}$ ins of bone; stallions have $7\frac{1}{4}$–9 ins. Haflingers are generally 13.1–14.2$\frac{1}{2}$ hh (135–148cm approx) with very placid temperaments.

There are classes for in-hand, ridden, dressage and driven Haflingers. The animals are shown in their natural state, as for native breeds.

The Haflinger is a popular riding and driving horse, shown here in traditional bridle and, as a purebred, unplaited.

The Haflinger Society of Great Britain is the governing body and all competitors should be members and their horses currently registered.

Haflingers

	Show or test	Ridden by judge	Plaited	English tack	Stripped	Trimming
Ridden	✓	optional	✗	any	✓	✗
In hand	✓	n/a	✗	plain	n/a	✗
Driven	✓	n/a	✗	✓	n/a	✗
Dressage	✓	n/a	✗†	✓	n/a	✗ but tidy

† Except affiliated BD classes, where it should be plaited as others.

Heavy Horses

The heavy horses are undoubtedly among the most spectacular animals to be seen in the show ring. The Shire, Clydesdale, Suffolk Punch and English Percheron are regularly shown throughout the country with a few Ardennes now joining them. Each has its own annual breed show.

The in-hand classes generally include those for mares (barren and in-foal), foals, yearlings, two- and three-year-olds, geldings, and occasionally stallions. There are often young handlers' classes, or prizes for these, as well as farriery competitions. Farriery and foot classes for Suffolks are particularly popular.

Harness classes include single and pairs with trade and agricultural vehicles. There are classes for teams of three, four and occasionally six. There are also classes for cleanest and best kept harness, and for decorated harness. Decorations vary in different parts of the country.

Each breed has a slightly different method of presentation – the Suffolk, for example, may have a full rig plait just under the crown of the mane intertwined with bass or wool and topped with coloured wool pom-poms. In-hand Suffolks are usually shown in leather halters.

Shires are often plaited with wool, bass or braid in a half rig plait into which 'flights' are incorporated (of an odd number). The Shire's knot on the tail is made with three separate strands of hair plaited under so that the 'bun' on top looks neat. A 'jug handle' or Yorkshire bob is often included, with two coloured ribbons added.

The Clydesdale usually has a tiny half rig plait along the top of the mane, which is braided. The flights, put in afterwards, should number eleven for in-hand classes and seven for harness. Percherons, like the Suffolks, have a full rig plait but on top of the neck and are fully braided with knotted tails. The colours most frequently used for braiding are red, yellow, blue, green, orange and white; and only two colours should ever be used together. The tails of foals are often braided but their manes are always left loose. Shaven tails are disliked by the public and are becoming less common.

Heavy Horses – In hand

	White rope halter	Braided manes and tails
Youngstock	✓**	✓†
Mares - barren and in foal	✓	✓
Geldings	✓	✓
Stallions/colts	✓*	✓

* Bit if required. ** Bridle with bit and harness. † Tails only for foals.

Heavy Horses – Driven

	White rope halter	Braided manes and tails
Trade	n/a	✓
Agricultural	n/a	✓
Decorative turnout	n/a	✓
Teams	n/a	✓

Clydesdale

The Clydesdale originates from Scotland where it has worked for many years on the farms and in the forests. Its colours are bay, brown, roan and occasionally black. A white stripe on the face, white markings on the underside of the body, and white stockings up to and over the knees and hocks are common. Its height ranges from 16.3hh to 18hh (170–183cm) and it is immensely strong; it is one of the world's most popular work horses. A distinguishing feature of the Clydesdale is the abundance of fine, silky feather on the legs. The Clydesdale moves with enormous energy, spring and power.

Today the Clydesdale is shown in heavy turnout classes and in hand.

The Clydesdale Horse Society of Great Britain and Ireland is the governing body.

A traditional sight at many of the bigger shows. Keeping the feather clean for show purposes requires a lot of dedication.

Percheron

The Percheron is a type of heavy draught horse originating from France from an area called La Perche. It is a particularly good-looking heavy horse and has enormous muscular development. It has ample bone and gives an impression of good balance and power. The Percheron varies in height from 16hh (163cm) to at least 18hh (183cm), and is either grey or black in colour. It moves very well for its size and despite its good temperament is not at all sluggish. With a fairly high influence of Arab in its original breeding there is a trace of elegance in this heavy horse.

Percherons are still used today for agricultural work and are shown and driven all over the world. One of the unusual features of the Percheron horse is that it has a very small amount of feather on the legs, i.e. clean-legged.

The British Percheron Society was formed in 1918 and is still the governing body for the breed.

The Percheron has less feather than most of the heavy breeds and its Arab ancestry is often obvious in the fineness of its head.

Shire Horse

The Shire horse originates from the Midlands and Fens in Britain. Permitted colours are black, bay, brown and grey. Shires stand up to 18hh (183cm) and over in height, and most have some white on their legs up to the knee and hock joint.

This huge horse has a remarkably docile temperament, and is often worked at three years old. In the past the Shire was used in industry, agriculture and transportation. Nowadays it is a popular show horse and draught worker for displays and brewery firms.

The Shire has a long, lean head with a slight Roman nose. The eyes are very docile in expression and the neck long and slightly arched. They have short legs with short cannons and a good amount of bone, up to 11ins. They have powerful and straight movement. A particular characteristic is the copious amount of silky feather on the legs.

Up to World War II, the Shire horse world was a male preserve but now there are a growing number of lady grooms/drivers.

The Shire Horse Society is the governing body.

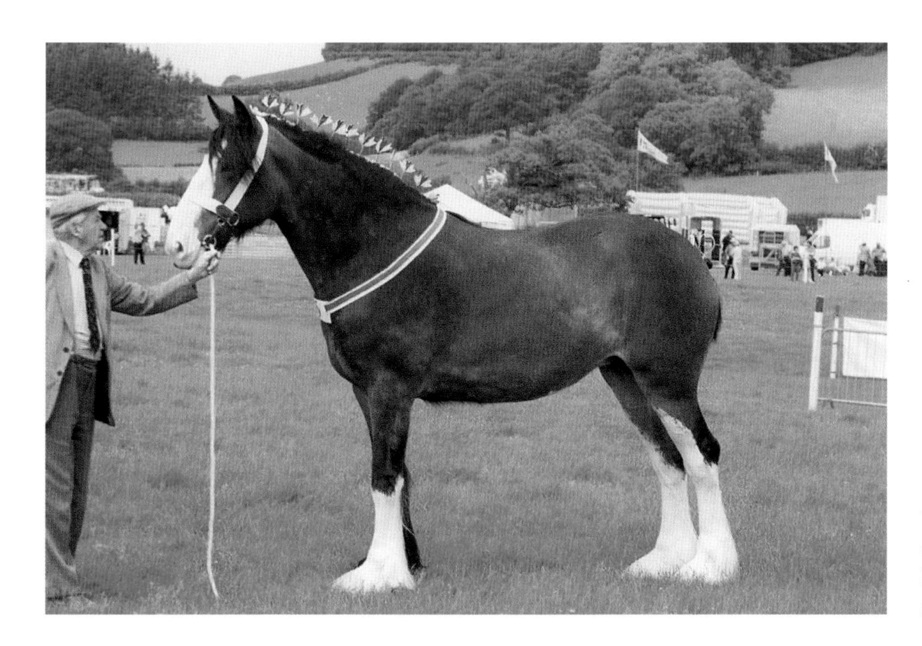

The Shire is generally the largest of the British gentle giants. Note the copious feather, spotlessly clean and silky.

SUFFOLK PUNCH

The Suffolk Punch originates from Suffolk and is thought to be the original war-horse. It is the purest British heavy breed and measures from 16hh (163cm) upwards. It is always chesnut (always spelt without the 't') with no markings except occasionally a small white star on the face. The seven chesnut colours vary in shade from light to dark, but by far the most common is bright chesnut. It has great width and is tremendously deep; it is enormously powerful and very well put together. It is considered most suitable for agricultural work, having very little feather.

The Suffolk Breed Society was formed in 1877 and is still the governing body for the breed.

This handsome Suffolk stallion is shown in a roller and side reins with crupper for greater control and presentation.

IRISH DRAUGHT

The Irish Draught was originally a farm horse in Ireland but its history is somewhat obscure. Usually it varies between 15hh (154cm) and 17hh (173cm) and is bay, brown, grey or chestnut with a small intelligent head. The body should be deep with a good shoulder, clean limbs with flat bone and strong but not overlarge feet. There should be no feather.

A stud book was started in Ireland in 1917 and in 1976 the Irish Draught Horse Society was formed to promote and preserve the breed. In 1979 the British Irish Horse Society was formed; it has introduced a strict inspection scheme for stallions and mares as well as a registration system. The Irish Draught has produced excellent competition horses when crossed with the Thoroughbred.

The Irish Draught has been influential in sport horse breeding and is a strong and versatile breed.

Irish Draught

	Individual show	Ridden by judge	Plaited	Plain browband	Stripped	Galloped	Trimmed
Ridden	✓	✓	✓	✓	✓	✓	✓
In hand	✓	✗	✓	✓	n/a	✗	not legs
Driven	✓	✗	✓	✓	n/a	✗	not legs
Small ridden	✓	✓	✓	✓	✓	✓	✓
Working hunter	✓	✓	✓	✓	✓	✓	✓
Part-bred	✓	✓	✓	✓	✓	✓	✓

NB: In 2004 a new class was introduced for pure and part-bred Irish Draught cobs not exceeding 15.2hh.

Cleveland Bay

The Cleveland Bay is one of the oldest British breeds. Originally used as pack horses they have since become outstanding carriage horses. They are often crossed with Thoroughbreds to produce top competition horses for all disciplines, and hunters with substance and quality.

Clevelands are very strong with characteristics to match. They are always bay in colour with black points. They possess good jumping ability and free, straight action. They should have a bold head carried on a long neck, and strong well-shaped feet which are blue in colour. Shallow or narrow feet are undesirable. Clevelands vary between 15hh and 17hh (154–173cm) and are shown in hand and ridden, as well as driven.

The Cleveland Bay Horse Society is the governing body.

Cleveland Bay

	Individual show	Ridden by judge	Plaited	Plain browband	Stripped	Galloped	Trimmed
Ridden*	✓	✓	✓	✓	✓	✓	✓
In hand	✓	✗	✓	✓	✓	✗	✓
Driven	✓	n/a	✓	driving	✗	✗	✓

* Judged as hunter class

Cleveland Bays are declining in numbers, despite their popularity as a cross for sport horses and use in carriage driving.

AMERICAN HORSES

The American horse has become increasingly popular in Britain and the three main breeds – the Morgan Horse, the Quarter Horse and the Saddlebred – have their own set of rules for in-hand and ridden classes, though the latter have been somewhat modified to suit British standards.

Western riding is now very popular and there are classes catering for Western pleasure horses, Western horsemanship, Western riding pattern, trail horses, stock horses, reining patterns, versatility (Western and English) and cattle roping. There are three Western rule books used in the UK and although each has slight variations the principles are similar.

In-hand classes are open to all breeds as it is the handler being judged rather than the horse, but horses must be in show condition (it is the rider who is being judged in the Western horsemanship classes also).

The governing bodies for American horses and Western riding include: the British Morgan Horse Society, the British Quarter Horse Association, the American Saddlebred Association of Great Britain, the Western Horseman's Association of Great Britain, American Quarter Horse Association, and the Western Equestrian Society.

QUARTER HORSE

The Quarter Horse possesses tremendous power in its hindquarters, with its hocks placed well underneath it, and is considered the fastest horse over a quarter-mile sprint. It is extremely agile, with a wonderful temperament

Quarter Horses are one of the most popular American breeds, with an easy temperament and tremendous speed. They are very popular as Western riding horses.

and its versatility has resulted in its being the most numerous breed in the USA. It usually stands between 14.3hh (150cm) and 16hh (163cm).

The British Quarter Horse Association Ltd is the governing body.

Quarter Horses

	Individual show	Ridden by judge	Plaited	Western tack	Stripped	Hand galloped	Dress
Ridden	✓	✗	✗	✓	✗	✗	traditional Western
Halter	✓	✗	✗	✓	✗	✗	
Western pleasure	✓	✗	✗	✓	✗	✗	
Western trail	✓	✗	✗	✓	✗	✗	
Western riding	✓	✗	✗	✓	✗	✗	
Reining	✓	✗	✗	✓	✗	✗	
Hunter hack	✓	✗	✗	✓	✗	✗	
Equitation	✓	✗	✗	✓	✗	✗	
Western horsemanship	✓	✗	✗	✓	✗	✗	

NB: Apply to breed societies for correct traditional dress code.

AMERICAN SADDLEBRED

The American Saddlebred is America's premier show horse and national breed. It was developed by the cotton plantation owners from the now extinct Old English Ambler and the Thoroughbred, and soon gained fame for its intelligent, courageous attitude, and fast, smooth gaits.

American Saddlebred

	Ridden by judge	Single braid (plait)	Double bridle	Coloured patent browband	Stripped	Hogged – 6–8″ back from ears	Trimmed
English hunt seat	opt. ✗	✓	✓	✓	✗	✓	✓
Mares	✗	✓	✓	✓	✗	✓	✓
Stallions	✗	✓	✓	✓	✗	✓	✓
Part-bred	✗	✓	✓	✓	✗	✓	✓
American saddle seat	✗	✓	✓	✓	✗	✓	✓
5-gaited	✗	✓	✓	✓	✗	✓	✓
3-gaited	✗	✓	✓	✓	✗	✓	✓
Youngsters in hand	✗	✓	✗	✓	✗	✓	✓

It is shown in USA tradition with the high neck carriage, flexed poll, elevated knees and hocks; imported five-gaited individuals also perform the slow-gait and 35mph rack. The rider wears a 'saddle suit' – flared trousers, frock coat and soft Derby hat. The horse is shown in the US saddle-seat style, in a double bridle with coloured patent leather browband matching the girth. The Saddlebred sports a flowing tail and mane with an extended bridle path to show off its flexion. Plaited ribbon is braided into the first lock of mane and into the forelock and then wrapped around the cheekpiece. It stands between 15hh (154cm) and 17hh (173cm) and can be found in all colours.

The governing body in the UK is the American Saddlebred Association of Great Britain.

Morgan Horse

The Morgan Horse is the oldest of America's light breeds. It originated from the small bay colt Figure, renamed Justin Morgan after his owner. Tough, agile, hardy and extremely fast, his progeny carried his strong characteristics which have changed remarkably little over the last two centuries. The breed has good conformation, is compact, well muscled and stylish. Its high, proud head carriage gives the impression of the neck sitting on top of the withers.

The governing body for Morgans is the British Morgan Horse Society.

Morgan

	Show	Ridden by judge	Mane plaited	Plain browband double bridle	Stripped	Hand galloped	Trimmed
Ridden	✗	✗	✗	✓	✗	✓	✓
In hand	✓	✗	✗	✗	✗	n/a	✓
Driven – 2/4 wheel	✗	✗	✗	✗	✗	n/a	✓
Pleasure	✗	✗	✗	✓	✗	n/a	✓
Park	✗	✗	✗	✓	✗	n/a	✓

NB: **Driving** – 2-wheeled buggy; **Park** – for higher action horses; **Pleasure** – for lower action horses.

Nordic Breeds

Icelandic Horse

Icelandic horses, which not surprisingly originate from Iceland, vary in height from 12–14hh (122–143cm). Most colours are found but the most common are dun and chestnut, including liver chestnut, with a flaxen mane and tail. They are very tough little ponies and many are exported; large numbers have been used as pit ponies in Britain. The Icelandic horse makes an ideal family mount and is used widely in disabled riding on account of its excellent temperament.

Icelandic horses are shown but they are ridden in classes designed only to show the purity and quality of the gaits. The classes may include the four-gait class, which shows walk, trot, canter and tolt (a four-beat running walk). Sometimes there are pace tests where horses can reach up to 30 miles an hour. The Icelandic is not judged on looks but on ability as a riding horse and on its temperament and character.

The Icelandic is stocky with a large head, intelligent eyes, and a short muscular neck with a thick mane. The body is compact, the quarters sloping and the limbs short and strong.

The Icelandic Horse Society is the governing body.

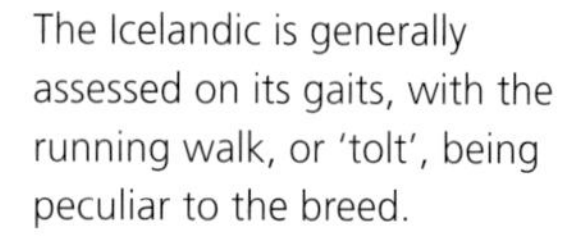

The Icelandic is generally assessed on its gaits, with the running walk, or 'tolt', being peculiar to the breed.

Icelandic

	Individual show	Ridden by judge	Plaited	Plain browband	Stripped	Galloped	Trimmed
Ridden	✓	✓	✓	✓	✓	✗	✗
In hand	✗	✗	✗	✓	✗	✗	✗
Driven	✗	✗	✗	optional	✗	✗	✗

NB: Marks given for breeding assessment, show, gaits, equitation.

FJORD HORSES

The Fjord horse originates from Norway, although now it is found extensively in Scandinavia. Its height varies from 13.2–14.2hh (138–148cm) and its only coat colour is sandy. Its distinctive feature is its mane, which is blond on the outside and has a black stripe running up the inside. The mane is trimmed with the blond part being cut 1in. (2.5cm) shorter than the black part.

The Fjord horse has a long history as a work-horse, being used centuries ago by the Vikings; today it is still used for logging in Norway and all over Scandinavia. It is now bred for riding and driving and a lot of horses compete in dressage competitions. Fjords are often accepted into mountain and moorland classes although some smaller shows exclude them since they are not native to Britain. They are shown trimmed and not plaited.

The Fjord Horse Society is the governing body.

Fjord

<table>
<tr><th></th><th>Individual show</th><th>Ridden by judge</th><th>Plaited</th><th>Plain browband</th><th>Stripped</th><th>Galloped</th><th>Trimmed</th></tr>
<tr><td>Ridden</td><td>✓</td><td>optional</td><td rowspan="3">✗ traditional cut</td><td>optional</td><td>optional</td><td>optional</td><td>optional</td></tr>
<tr><td>In hand</td><td>✓</td><td>✗</td><td>optional</td><td>optional</td><td>✗</td><td>optional</td></tr>
<tr><td>Driven</td><td>✓</td><td>✗</td><td>optional</td><td>optional</td><td>✗</td><td>optional</td></tr>
</table>

THE FALABELLA AND OTHER MINIATURE HORSES

This relatively new breed, which originates from Argentina, is one of the world's smallest, standing less than 8.2hh (86cm). Falabellas have the appearance of scaled-down horses and are generally kept as pets. They take two to three generations to scale down to the required size. They are occasionally driven, or led in halter classes, or jumped in hand.

The International Falabella Miniature Horse Society is responsible for that particular breed.

Other miniature horses, such as Miniature Shetlands, Arabs, etc. are also evolving, and are catered for by the British Miniature Horse Society (BMHS), which is at present a height register for anything under 34 inches (about 86 cms) at the wither. There are qualifying shows around the UK with various in-hand performance classes.

Falabellas and Other Miniature Horses

	Show	Ridden by judge	Plaited	Plain browband	Stripped	Galloped	Trimmed
In hand	✗	✗	✗	✓	n/a	n/a	✗ (tidy)
Halter	as handy pony	✗	✗	✓	n/a	n/a	✗ (tidy)
Jumping	in hand	✗	✗	✓	n/a	n/a	✗ (tidy)

Caspian Horse

Normally between 10–12.2hh (101–128cm) the Caspian gives the appearance of a well-bred elegant horse in miniature. It has a fine, silky coat with the mane and tail of a Thoroughbred but the winter coat of a mountain pony. Caspians have a calm, alert and willing temperament and are very intelligent. They are extremely strong, jump well and are highly suitable as riding, driving and jumping ponies.

The British Caspian Society deals with all registrations, memberships, etc. and runs its own breed show.

Caspian Horses

	Individual show	Ridden by judge	Plaited	Plain browband	Stripped	Galloped	Trimmed
Ridden	✓	✓	✗	✓	✓	✗	discreet
In hand	✓	n/a	✗	✓	n/a	✗	discreet
Driven	✓	n/a	✗	✓	n/a	✗	discreet
Special children's classes	✓	✗	✗	✓	✓	✗	discreet

DONKEYS

Donkeys are great favourites and are shown in the same way as other equines. There is an annual championship show for them with several qualifiers held around the country. Open or private driving classes are sometimes split into classes for private driving and exercise vehicles. Ridden classes for children are restricted by a height/weight ratio depending on the size of the donkey to give a good overall picture. For example, 4ft and 8 stone is the limit for a 10.2hh (106cm) donkey and 5ft and 9 stone is the limit for a 12hh (122cm) donkey.

Because of their thick coats and love of rolling, donkeys generally require a good bath before showing, weather permitting. Driven donkeys are sometimes trace-clipped in hot weather.

There are often prizes for the Best Young Handler, Junior Whip, Novice Donkey, etc. The Donkey Breed Society is the governing body.

Donkey classes require professional presentation, as with any other class. Ask for tips from the professionals to ensure you and your donkey are correctly turned out.

Donkeys

	Individual show	Safety hat	Bit required	Show bridle/ headcollar	Trimmed mane*
In-hand stallions/colts	✓	optional	✓	✓	✓
In-hand geldings	✓	optional	✗	✓	✓
In-hand mares	✓	optional	✗	✓	✓
In-hand youngstock (yearling, 2 & 3 yrs)	✓	optional	optional	✓	✓
Ridden	✓	✓	✓	✓	✓
Driven	✓	n/a	✓	driving tack	✓
Young handler	✓	✓	✓	✓	✓

* Manes are generally trimmed to one and half inches so that they 'stand up'. Tails are trimmed to look tidy. Hooves are oiled.

VETERAN HORSES AND PONIES

The older horse is at last being recognised as well capable of continuing to do a job. Veteran classes are becoming increasingly popular, catering for Pre-Veterans aged 15-19 years and Veterans 20-29 years, with a Golden Veteran section for those of 30 years or above. There are also novice classes for 15 years and over, and the classes cater for both ponies not exceeding 14.2hh and horses over 14.2hh.

The classes are judged on the animal's condition in relation to its age, its alertness and zest for life, freedom of movement, suppleness and regularity of pace. The age of the horse must be displayed on the bridle. There is no galloping or jumping in these classes and spurs should not be worn. The condition and turnout of the horse and rider are taken into account, and the classes are judged on a marks system which includes the following:

- The walk, trot and canter
- Condition and overall appearance
- Turnout
- Manners and personality

There are also performance awards aimed at encouraging older horses to participate, and classes cater for stallions, mares and geldings.

The governing body is the Veteran Horse Society.

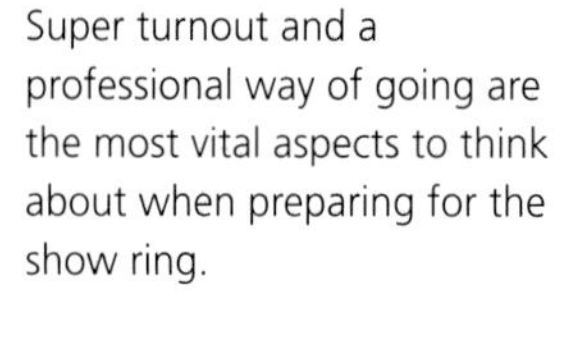

Super turnout and a professional way of going are the most vital aspects to think about when preparing for the show ring.

Veteran Horses

	Turnout*	Age displayed	Plaited	Ridden by judge	Galloping/ jumping	Spurs
Ridden**	tidy	✓	✓	✗	✗	✗
In hand	tidy	✓	✓	n/a	n/a	n/a

NB: Marks are not deducted for old injuries or scars, so long as complete recovery has taken place.

* Turnout is as for hunters or riding horses, with the emphasis on neatness and presentation.

** An individual show for ridden sections is, generally, required.

Amateur and Unaffiliated Classes

Alongside all the affiliated shows run by showing and breed associations, are a mass of unaffiliated shows catering for every type of horse and pony, with a myriad different classes to suit everyone. These shows are, typically, put on by local riding clubs, hunts, pony clubs, or charitable organisations. They are usually there to raise money for their own organisation or a good cause, and so tend to be very cost-effectively administered, with the minimum of facilities and lots of classes, often in several different rings. They involve huge amounts of hard work and fun for all those participating.

At unaffiliated shows one can generally find a variety of showing classes, including those for ponies, hunters, riding horses, veterans, amateur riders, local, coloured, in-hand and sometimes dressage. Even if your horse or pony is not a breed specimen or show type there are still classes you can enter, such as 'Best turned out', 'Family horse/pony', 'Young handler', 'First pony', to name but a few.

In addition there may well be several jumping classes, which could include clear round, minimus and/or leading rein, as well as bigger courses for the more ambitious.

Most of these classes are run along the lines of the regulations for the relevant affiliated classes but adapted to suit the standard of the show. The schedule will generally stipulate how the classes will be conducted. However, individual judges may decide to vary things a little, depending on the number in the class, the timetable, the weather, and so on. In some classes they may ride the exhibits, so make sure you know if this is likely to be the case.

Two well-turned out riders who have obviously been successful. These two are unplaited for their respective classes, but many show classes require the exhibits to be plaited. Check with an experienced person how you should present for the various classes.

In all showing classes, neatness and turnout of horse and rider play a big part alongside the way the animal performs, so watch those who know the form and learn from them. The better you fulfil the criteria required, the greater your chance of success.

Plaiting is obviously important for most showing classes (except for the mountain and moorland classes) but if you are just tackling the jumping classes, it is not essential to plait up. However, your horse or pony should always be well turned out, cleaned and trimmed appropriately.

Neatness and tidiness of the rider is equally as important as that of your mount. Tweed jackets always look good, although blue, black, and brown are now much more common in unaffiliated shows. Any brightly coloured hat silks, numnahs or boots should be left at home. The professionals always keep everything discreet so that their horse or pony catches the judge's eye.

Most shows expect hats with a safety harness to be worn at all times and may stipulate that back-protectors should be worn in jumping classes, especially by children.

Entries are generally accepted on the day at the secretary's office where you collect your number, usually one number per horse, regardless of the number of classes you enter. Some shows will only accept entries sent before the day, so check carefully on the schedule. There is often a queue at the secretary's tent, so allow plenty of time if you want to compete in early classes, and always keep an eye on the ring so you are ready for your class. The timetable at these shows is often difficult to predict because of uncertainty over numbers, so the onus is on the competitor to be ready.

Some shows hold qualifiers for different area or regional championships and one of these, 'Search for a Star', is becoming particularly prestigious. 'Search for a Star' is designed to give amateur owners and riders an opportunity to compete at the Horse of the Year Show, currently held at the National Exhibition Centre, Birmingham in September/October.

Horses and ponies suitable as a working hunter, riding club show horse, show ponies, show hunter ponies, cobs, show hunters, riding horses and hack are all eligible. Selection days are held around the country, generally between June and August, following the accepted showing routine for those classes. Two entries, providing they reach a good show standard, are invited to take part in the final.

Useful Addresses

American Quarter Horse Association of Great Britain
7 Whitehall Way
Sellindge
Ashford
KENT
TN25 6ET
tel: 01303 814879
www.aqha.co.uk

American Saddlebred Association of Great Britain
Uplands
Alfriston
East Sussex
BN26 5XE
tel: 01323 870977
www. americansaddlebreds.co.uk

Anglo-European Studbook
PO Box 75
Crowborough
East Sussex
TN6 1ZT
tel: 01892 610155
www.angloeuropeanstudbook.ltd.uk

Arab Horse Society
Windsor House
The Square
Ramsbury
Marlborough
Wiltshire
SN8 2PE
tel: 01672 520782
www.arabhorsesoc-uk.com

British Appaloosa Society
31 Navigators Way
Hedge End
Gosport
Southampton
SO30 2GP
tel: 01489 785577
www.appaloosa.org.uk

British Association for the Purebred Spanish Horse
Church Farm
Church Street
Semington
Wiltshire
BA14 6JS
tel: 01380 871873
www.bapsh.co.uk

British Bavarian Warmblood Association
Sittyton
Straloch
Newmacher
Aberdeenshire
AB21 0RP
tel: 01651 882226
www.bbwa.co.uk

British Driving Society
27 Dugard Place
Barford
Warwick
CV35 8DX
tel: 01926 624420
www.britishdrivingsociety.co.uk

British Hanoverian Horse Society
Ecton Fields Plantation
Ecton Lane
Sywell
Northampton
NN6 0BP
tel: 01604 492750
www.hanoverian-gb.org.uk

British Horse Society
Stoneleigh Deer Park
Kenilworth
Warwickshire
CV8 2XZ
tel: 08701 202244
www.bhs.org.uk

British Miniature Horse Society
Zeals House
Lower Zeals
Warminster
Wiltshire
BA12 6LG
tel: 01747 861619
www.bmhs.co.uk

British Morgan Horse Society
PO Box 155
Godalming
Surrey
GU8 5YE
tel: 01483 861283
www.morganhorse.org.uk

British Palomino Society
Penrhiwllan
Llandysul
Dyfed
SA44 5NZ
tel: 01239 851387
www.britishpalominosociety.co.uk

British Percheron Horse Society
Three Bears Cottage
Burston Road
Diss
Norfolk
IP22 5UF
tel: 01379 740554
www.percheron.org.uk

British Show Hack, Cob and Riding Horse Association
2 High Street
Hitchin
Herts
SG5 1BH
tel: 01462 437770
www.showhackandcob.org.uk

British Show Pony Society
124 Green End Road
Sawtry
Huntingdon
Cambridgeshire
PE28 5XS
tel: 01487 831376
www.britishshowponysociety.co.uk

British Skewbald and Piebald Association
PO Box 67
Ely
Cambridgeshire
CB7 4FY
tel: 01354 638226
www.bspaonline.com

British Sports Horse Register
Lower Tredenham
Lanibet
Bodmin
Cornwall
PL30 5HL
tel: 01208 832940

British Warmblood Society
Lower Tredenham
Lanibet
Bodmin
Cornwall
PL30 5HL
tel: 01208 832940

Caspian Horse Society
6 Nuns Walk
Virginia Water
Surrey
GU25 4RT
tel: 01344 843325
www.caspianhorsesociety.org.uk

Cleveland Bay Horse Society
York Livestock Centre
Murton
York
Y19 5GF
tel: 01904 489731
www.clevelandbay.com

Clydesdale Horse Society of Great Britain and Ireland
Castlepark
The Castleton
Auchterarder
Perthshire
PH3 1JR
tel: 01764 664327
www.clydesdalehorse.co.uk

Coloured Horse and Pony Society (UK)
1 McLaren Cottages
Abertysswg
Rhymney
Tredegar
Blaenau
Gwent
NP22 5BH
tel: 01685 845045
www.chapsuk.com

Dales Pony Society
Greystones
Glebe Avenue
Great Logstone
Bakewell
Derbyshire
DE45 1TY
tel: 01629 640439
www.dalespony.org

Dartmoor Pony Society
Forge Cottage
65 High Street
Warboys
Cambridge
PE28 2TA
tel: 01487 822635
www.dartmoorponysociety.com

Donkey Breed Society
The Hermitage
Pootings
Edenbridge
Kent
TN8 6SD
tel: 01732 864414
www.donkeybreedsociety.co.uk

British Connemara Pony Society
Glen Farm
Waddicombe
Dulverton
Somerset
TA22 9RY
tel: 01398 341490
www.britishconnemaras.co.uk

European Committee of the Arab Horse Organisation
The General Secretary of ECAHO
Entenstrasse 20
D-73765
Neuhausen/F
Germany
tel: + 49 7158 67141
www.ecaho.org

Exmoor Pony Society
Glen Farm
Waddicombe
Dulverton
Somerset
TA22 9RY
tel: 01398 341490
www.exmoorponysociety.org.uk

Fell Pony Society
North Craigs Cottage
Waterbeck
Lockerbie
Dumfriesshire
DG11 3HA
tel: 01461 600606
www.raresteeds.com/fellponysociety

Fjord Horse National Stud Book Association of Great Britain, The
Cilyblaidd Manor
Near Lampeter
Pencarreg
Carmarthenshire
SA40 9QL
tel: 01570 480090
www.fjord-horse.co.uk

Friesian Horse Association of Great Britain & Ireland, The
Harbours Hill Farm
Hanbury Road
Stoke Prior
Worcestershire
B60 4AG
tel: 01977 602232
www.fhagbi.co.uk

Hackney Horse Society
Fallowfields
Little London
Heytesbury
Warminster
Wiltshire
BA12 0ES
tel: 01985 840 717
www.hackney-horse.org.uk

Haflinger Society of Great Britain, The
Wayside Cottage
2 The Hopground
Finchingfield
Essex
CM7 4LU
tel: 01761 490923
www.haflingersgb.com

Highland Pony Society, The
22 York Place
Perth
PH2 8EH
tel: 01738 451861
www.highland-pony.demon.co.uk

Icelandic Horse Society of Great Britain, The
8 Brown Court
Grangemouth
FK3 9LU
tel: 01324 411090
www.ihsgb.freeserve.co.uk

International Falabella Miniature Horse Society
Holding
The Barracks
Hook
Hampshire
RG27 9NW
tel: 01256 763425
www.falabella.co.uk

Irish Draught Horse Society (GB), The
PO Box 1869
Salisbury
Wiltshire
SP3 5XA
tel: 08452 300399 / 01722 714970
www.irishdraughthorsesociety.com

Joint Measurement Board Limited
Westcoats Farm
Stanhill
Charlwood
Surrey
RH6 0ES
tel: 01293 862101
www.thejmbonline.co.uk

Lipizzaner Society of Great Britain
Starrock Stud
Ludwell
Shaftsbury
Dorset
SP7 0PW
tel: 01747 828639
www.lipizzaner.co.uk

Lusitano Breed Society (Great Britain), The
Hooper's Oak
Woolhope
Herefordshire
HR1 4RQ
tel: 01531 660289
www.lbsgb.co.uk

National Pony Society
Willingdon House
102 High Street
Alton
Hampshire
GU34 1EN
tel: 01420 88333
www.nationalponysociety.org.uk

New Forest Pony Breeding and Cattle Society, The
The Corner House
Ringwood Road
Bransgore
Hampshire, BH23 8AA
tel: 01425 672775
www.newforestpony.com

Ponies UK
Chesham House
56 Green End Road
Sawtry
Huntingdon
Cambridgeshire
PE28 5UA
tel: 01487 830278
www.poniesuk.org

Pony Club, The
NAC Stoneleigh Park
Kenilworth
Warwickshire
CV8 2RW
tel: 02476 698300
www.pony-club.org.uk

Shetland Pony Stud Book Society, The
Shetland House
22 York Place
Perth
PH2 8EH
tel: 01738 623471
www.shetlandponystudbooksociety.co.uk

Shire Horse Society
East of England Showground
Peterborough
Cambridgeshire
PE2 6XE
tel: 01733 234451
www.shire-horse.org.uk

Side Saddle Association, The
Nightingale Cottage
Coedyr-Eos
Valentine Road
Abersychan
Pontypool
NP4 8QP
tel: 01495 772212
www.equiworld.com/ssa

Sport Horse Breeding of Great Britain
96 Highstreet
Edenbridge
Kent
TN8 5AR
tel: 01732 866277
www.sporthorsegb.co.uk

Spotted Pony Breed Society of Great Britain
Tollbar Cottage
Butterley Park
Rippley
Derbyshire
DE5 3QW
tel: 01773 748502

Suffolk Horse Society
The Market Hill
Woodbridge
Suffolk
IP12 4LU
tel: 01394 380643
www.suffolkhorsesociety.org.uk

Thoroughbred Breeders Association
Stanstead House
The Avenue
Newmarket
Suffolk
CB8 9AA
tel: 01638 661321
www.thoroughbredbreedersassociation.co.uk

Trakehner Breeders Fraternity
Bluewood Stud
Lower Lidham Hill Farm
North Lane
Guestling
East Sussex
TN35 4LX
tel: 0870 432 5075
www.trakehnerbreeders.com

Veteran Horse Society
Hendre Fawr Farm
St Dogmaels
Cardigan
SA43 3LZ
tel: 01239 881300
www.veteran-horse-society.co.uk

Weatherbys
Sanders Road
Wellingborough
Northants
NN8 4BX
tel: 01933 440077
www.weatherbys-group.com

Welsh Pony and Cob Society
6 Chalybeate Street
Aberystwyth
Ceredigion
SY23 1HP
tel: 01970 617501
www.wpcs.uk.com

Western Equestrian Society
20 Newlands Close
Yately
Hampshire
GU46 6HE
tel: 01252 875896
www.wes-uk.com

Western Horseman's Association of Great Britain
3 Poplar Close
High Cross
Hertfordshire
SG11 1AY
tel: 01920 486182
www.westernhorsemanofgb.co.uk

Index

Page numbers in **bold** refer to illustrations